CONTENTS

Special Bonus 1

Introduction 2

1: Unveiling the Mystery: Hello, Puberty! 3

2: The Amazing World of Hormones 8

3: Rollercoaster Ride: Embracing Mood Swings 14

4: The ABCs of Periods 18

5: Pimples, Zits, and Other Skin Surprises 23

6: Growing Pains: Navigating Body Changes 28

7: Let's Talk Bras: Finding the Perfect Fit 33

8: Hair Today, Gone Tomorrow: A Guide to Body Hair ... 37

9: The Monthly Visitor: Dealing with Periods 43

10: Cracking the Code of Cramps 50

11: PMS SOS: Taming the Monthly Beast 57

12: The Science Behind Menstruation 62

13: Puberty Power: Discovering Your Strength 67

14: Healthy Habits for a Happy Body 72

15: The Mirror Challenge: Building Self-Confidence ... 77

16: Friends Forever: Navigating Social Changes 82

17: Crush Chronicles: Navigating Relationships 87

18: Cyber Space: Navigating Social Media 92

19: #BodyPositivity: Loving Your Unique Self 98

20: Food Fuel: Eating Right for Puberty 103

21: Sleep Secrets: Beauty Rest for Growing Bodies ... 109

22: Stress Busters: Coping with the Teen Tornado 114

23: Parent-Teen Talks: Building Bridges 119

24: Celebrating You: Embracing Individuality 126

25: Beyond Puberty: A Sneak Peek into the Future 130

Conclusion 135

Special Bonus 136

Thnak You 137

SPECIAL BONUS

Want this bonus book for free?

SKILLS and be the first to claim a free download of our upcoming releases.

Scan the QR CODE  Join Today!

INTRODUCTION

Welcome, Adventurer! Embark on the Journey of You!

Hey there, incredible being! Are you ready for an epic adventure? Buckle up because you're about to embark on the most exciting quest of all: exploring the amazing world within you! This book isn't just a guide; it's a treasure map leading you through the wonders of puberty, a transformative time bursting with growth, change, and, yes, maybe even a few bumps along the way.

Think of yourself as a fearless adventurer, ready to conquer dragons (okay, perhaps they're more like metaphorical dragons of self-doubt), navigate uncharted territories (like understanding your changing body), and discover hidden treasures (like your unique strengths and passions). Don't worry, you're not alone! We'll be your trusty companions, offering honest advice, sharing relatable stories, and cheering you on every step of the way.

Forget boring lectures and stuffy textbooks. This book is packed with fun, humor, and real talk because growing up shouldn't feel like a chore. We'll tackle everything from physical changes and emotional rollercoasters to navigating friendships, managing stress, and celebrating your amazing individuality.

So, are you ready to unlock the magic within?

1

UNVEILING THE MYSTERY: HELLO, PUBERTY!

Once upon a time, a group of fearless and fabulous girls discovered the enchanted path of self-discovery in the magical land of Growing Up. Just like you, these girls were on the brink of a magnificent adventure called puberty. As they navigated the twists and turns of this uncharted territory, they stumbled upon the secret to unlocking their true potential and becoming the heroines of their own stories.

Guess what? You're about to embark on a super cool adventure in the land of Growing Up! Just like some awesome girls before you, you're heading into a magical journey called puberty. It's like discovering a secret path to find out more about yourself and becoming the superhero of your own story!

Picture this: you're standing at the entrance of a world full of changes, challenges, and tons of chances to grow. This journey isn't just any trip; it's your very own Unstoppable Journey! Imagine it like a super exciting quest where you hold the key to unlock the magic within you.

No boring lectures or boring facts here! We're diving into this adventure together through tales of friendship, courage, and discovering who you are. It's like your very own fairy tale, with you as the brave hero ready to face anything that comes your way.

As we go through the chapters, we'll solve the mysteries of puberty with stories that are all about you – the incredible girl you are. From the changes happening inside your body to the superpowers that come with embracing your uniqueness – every chapter is a step on your way to becoming the awesome person you're meant to be.

So, grab your imaginary sword of confidence, put on your crown of self-love, and let's start this adventure together! Your Unstoppable Journey is about to unfold, and the magic within you is going to shine in the most amazing ways! Are you ready to find the hero within? Let the adventure begin!

Now, let me tell you about our brave heroines in the Enchanted Forest:

The Blooming Meadow of Curves

Our heroines found a beautiful meadow where flowers bloomed along with the curves appearing on their bodies. It was a magical dance of hormones – estrogen and progesterone – making them grow and transform. "Just like the flowers, your curves are a natural part of your beautiful journey," said a wise old tree.

The Mirror of Self-Discovery

Our heroines stumbled upon a magical mirror reflecting their physical changes and the blossoming of their unique personalities. "Embrace the reflection you see, for it's the result of the incredible person you are becoming," echoed the mirror, showing the natural and gradual evolution happening within.

The River of Emotions

Navigating through the Enchanted Forest, our heroines found the River of Emotions flowing with feelings from joy to uncertainty. "Emotions are like the river's current – sometimes calm, sometimes turbulent, but always a part of the natural ebb and flow of life," whispered the river.

The Cave of Friendship

Deep within the forest, our heroines discovered the Cave of Friendship. As they shared their experiences, they realized each girl's journey was unique yet connected. "Friendship is the lantern that lights up the darkest corners of puberty. Together, you can face anything," advised mystical creatures in the cave.

Starry Skies of Self-Love

Under the starlit sky, our heroines gathered around a magical fire reflecting the glow of self-love. "Just as the stars shine brightly, so does the light within you. Embrace every part of yourself, for it is the source of your greatest power," whispered the night breeze.

The Natural Magic Unveiled

Throughout their quest, our heroines discovered everything they were experiencing was part of a natural and beautiful process. Puberty wasn't a curse or a mysterious spell; it was the unfolding of their own unique stories.

You, dear reader, are also part of this magical journey! Every change, emotion, and discovery is an entirely natural and normal part of growing up. The Enchanted Forest of Changes reminds you that you're not alone – the natural magic of puberty surrounds you, and it's a story uniquely yours.

And now, let's be honest, and let me tell you that whatever changes you might go through are nothing to be embarrassed or confused about. It is all a natural process that every girl around your age goes through or will go through. Feeling excited about growing up, experiencing new things, and discovering more about yourself is perfectly normal. It's like starting a new chapter in the book of your life, and that excitement is a sign of the positive changes that await you.

Being curious about the changes happening in your body and wanting to understand them is entirely natural. Curiosity is like a friendly guide, leading you to discover the wonders of puberty and helping you navigate this exciting journey. Feeling a bit nervous or unsure about what's to come is totally okay. It's like stepping into the unknown, and everyone, at some point, has felt a bit nervous about changes. Remember, it's okay not to have all the answers right away.

Although, don't forget everything can be fun too. Experiencing moments of joy and happiness, especially when surrounded by friends or discovering new things about yourself, is a beautiful part of growing up. Embracing these joyful moments is a celebration of your unique journey.

Feeling a bit confused or overwhelmed by the changes is completely normal. Puberty is a time of transformation, and it's okay if things seem a bit confusing at first. You have the power to navigate through it, and clarity will come with time.

Seeking comfort and support from friends or family during this time is a natural instinct. Sharing experiences and realizing that others might feel the same way can create strong bonds. Friendship is like a guiding light through the twists and turns of puberty.

Discovering more about yourself, your interests, and your strengths is an exciting part of this journey. Embracing self-discovery allows you to celebrate the unique qualities that make you who you are. Being patient with yourself is also key. Stuff is changing, and it may be changing too fast, but you have to be patient about it. Changes take time, and it's completely normal to feel impatient at moments. Remember, your journey unfolds naturally; patience is your ally during this adventure.

Realizing that you have the power to shape your own story is an empowering feeling. Embrace the superhero within because you are the heroine of your own tale and have the strength to face anything that comes your way.

Loving yourself is another crucial aspect, including all the changes happening in your body and mind and it is a crucial aspect of this journey. Just like the stars shining brightly in the sky, you being you makes the world a better and more exciting place.

2

THE AMAZING WORLD OF HORMONES

Hey there, future hormone experts! Welcome to the exciting world of hormones, where your body becomes a bustling playground of incredible changes and super cool transformations. Get ready to dive into the mysteries of estrogen and progesterone – the dynamic duo that makes puberty the extraordinary adventure it is!

Meet the Superheroes

Imagine hormones as the superheroes inside your body, working their magic to help you grow and become the fantastic person you're destined to be. Meet Estrogen, the leading lady, and Progesterone, her trusty sidekick. They're like the superheroes of the puberty world, creating the perfect team for your body's grand production.

The Hormone Dance

Picture your body as a lively dance floor; Estrogen and Progesterone are the star dancers. They perform a magical hormone dance, orchestrating the growth of your amazing features. Estrogen takes the lead in making your body bloom, like flowers in a spring garden, while Progesterone ensures everything stays in perfect harmony.

The Magical Hormone Dance

Together, Estrogen and Progesterone perform a magical hormone dance on the body's stage, orchestrating a symphony of growth and transformation. The dance is dynamic, intricate, and uniquely tailored to each individual, creating a beautiful and harmonious performance.

Just as every dancer brings their unique style to the dance floor, each person's hormone dance during puberty is unique. The rate and sequence of changes can vary, making your dance a one-of-a-kind masterpiece.

The hormone dance isn't a one-time performance; it's a journey that unfolds gradually. As your body matures, the dance continues, and the coordination between Estrogen and Progesterone ensures a seamless and beautiful progression.

Growth Spurts and Superpowers

Hold on tight for the rollercoaster ride of growth spurts! Estrogen signals your body to grow taller, and Progesterone ensures everything develops at the right pace. These changes are like acquiring superpowers – you're becoming stronger, more resilient, and ready to tackle anything that comes your way.

Have you ever wondered about those tiny visitors called pimples? They're like little storytellers, indicating that your skin is experiencing changes. Estrogen and Progesterone are working to ensure your skin becomes more resilient, just like a superhero's armor, as you navigate the adventure of puberty. Pimples, those small visitors that sometimes pop up on your skin, are like little messengers delivering a message about the changes happening underneath the surface. Think of them as storytellers, sharing a tale of your body's transformation during the adventure of puberty.

Now, let's get into the Story of Skin Changes…

During puberty, your body goes through a remarkable process of growth and development, and your skin is no exception. Estrogen and Progesterone, the superhero hormones, are actively involved in this story.

Estrogen, the leading lady in this hormone duo, works to make your skin more supple and soft. It helps your skin retain moisture, giving it a healthy and radiant appearance. However, as your body adjusts to the increased hormone levels, it might produce more oil in your skin glands.

Progesterone, the trusty sidekick, is also at work to support your skin's journey. It contributes to the production of sebum, an oily substance that helps keep your skin lubricated and protected. However, excess sebum can sometimes lead to clogged pores, creating an environment where pimples can appear.

Your skin is like a superhero's armor, and Estrogen and Progesterone are the crafting masters behind it. As your skin goes through changes, it becomes more resilient, adapting to the new levels of hormones and the increased oil production.

While the appearance of pimples might seem like a challenge, it's actually a sign that your skin is adapting and becoming more resilient. Your body is working to find the right balance of oil production, and the presence of pimples is a part of this process.

Just like a superhero's armor transforms to become stronger and more durable, your skin is evolving to face the challenges of puberty. Over time, as your body adjusts to the hormonal changes, your skin will likely become more balanced and clearer.

Remember, pimples are temporary guests on your skin, and their visit is a natural part of the puberty adventure. The key is to take care of your skin with gentle cleansing, a healthy diet, and regular skincare routines.

The Emotion Express

All aboard the Emotion Express!

Hormones also play a role in the emotional journey of puberty. Sometimes, you might feel like you're on a rollercoaster of different feelings. That's totally normal! Estrogen and Progesterone are just helping you express yourself and understand your emotions better. Feeling different emotions is like having a colorful palette of feelings, and it's all part of growing up.

Understanding these feelings helps you navigate through the exciting and sometimes challenging adventure of puberty.

The Menstrual Marvel or the "Period"

Here comes the super-heroic moment – the menstrual cycle!

Estrogen and Progesterone take center stage, preparing your body for the possibility of creating life someday.

It's like your body's way of getting ready for an incredible adventure in the future. The menstrual cycle is a natural part of growing up and becoming a young woman. It's a sign that your body is getting ready for amazing things in the future, even if it might initially feel a bit mysterious.

Hormones and Harmony

Just like a magical orchestra, your body is harmonizing with the help of these hormones. They're the conductors, ensuring everything is in tune, creating a beautiful symphony of growth and development. Embrace the changes, for they're all part of the amazing story of you. This harmony ensures that all the changes happening in your body are part of a natural and beautiful process.

Embracing these changes is like enjoying the music of your body and becoming the incredible person you're meant to be.

The Hormone Handbook

Remember, these superheroes, Estrogen and Progesterone, are your body's best friends during puberty. They're working hard to ensure you grow into the fantastic person you're meant to be. So, when you feel the hormone dance or experience the emotion expressed, know it's all part of the incredible adventure of becoming you!

Ready to rock the world of hormones?

3

ROLLERCOASTER RIDE: EMBRACING MOOD SWINGS

Welcome, fearless adventurers, to the wild world of mood swings – the rollercoaster of emotions during puberty. Imagine your feelings as a thrilling amusement park, with Estrogen and Progesterone as the magical conductors of this emotional symphony. Like puppeteers behind the scenes, these hormones create ups and downs in your emotions, akin to a rollercoaster ride. Understanding that these hormone levels fluctuate helps you navigate the emotional amusement park with the knowledge that mood swings are a normal part of growing up.

Just like a rollercoaster, mood swings have their highs and lows. Sometimes, you'll feel on top of the world, bursting with energy; other times, you might experience moments of feeling a bit down. Embracing these emotional fluctuations is like holding a ticket to the full spectrum of puberty's colorful journey. Riding the emotional rollercoaster allows you to develop resilience and adaptability, essential superpowers for life.

Just as any adventurer needs tools for their journey, you can have a toolkit to navigate the mood swing rollercoaster. Expressing yourself, taking *me-time* for enjoyable activities, and maintaining healthy habits become your coping strategies toolkit. These tools help you stay on track during the ups and downs, ensuring a smoother ride through puberty's emotional twists and turns.

Come and take a deep dive with me into what all these tools are:

1. Express Yourself:

Talking about your feelings is like shining a light on the rollercoaster's twists and turns. Whether it's with friends, family, or a trusted adult, sharing your emotions helps release any pent-up energy. It's okay not to have all the answers, and expressing yourself creates connections that make the journey less daunting.

2. Me-Time for Enjoyable Activities:

Imagine a pit stop in the amusement park where you can choose activities that bring joy and relaxation. Whether it's reading a favorite book, drawing, or listening to music, these activities become your emotional refueling station. Me-time is essential for recharging your emotional batteries and finding moments of calm amidst the rollercoaster ride.

3. Healthy Habits:

Your body is like a superhero preparing for an epic battle against mood swings. Eating well, getting enough sleep, and engaging in regular exercise are powerful tools in your arsenal. A balanced diet ensures your body gets the nutrients it needs, adequate sleep rejuvenates your energy, and exercise releases those feel-good hormones. These healthy habits provide stability and resilience against the ups and downs of the emotional rollercoaster.

Why These Tools Matter:

1. **Empowerment:** Expressing yourself empowers you to navigate emotions with a support system.
2. **Joyful Recharge:** Me-time activities bring joy, serving as a positive outlet during challenging moments.
3. **Stability and Resilience:** Healthy habits create a foundation of stability and resilience, helping you better withstand the twists and turns of mood swings.

Remember, this coping strategies toolkit is like a personalized guide for your emotional journey. As you become familiar with these tools, you gain the ability to steer through the rollercoaster of emotions with confidence and grace.

And I have another idea in mind…

What if you could document your rollercoaster adventure? Journaling becomes your personalized map through the twists and turns of emotions. Write down your thoughts, experiences, and even the highs and lows of the day. Journaling helps you understand patterns, providing insights into what triggers certain emotions and how you can better navigate them. It's like having a secret diary where your emotions come to life, and you hold the pen to your unique story.

Sometimes, even the bravest adventurers need a guide through the rollercoaster's labyrinth. Seeking professional support, like talking to a counselor or therapist, is like having a seasoned navigator by your side. They offer tools and strategies tailored to your unique experience, helping you gain a deeper understanding of your emotions and providing valuable insights for a smoother ride.

Incorporating these additional tools into your coping strategies toolkit provides even more resources for your emotional journey. Just as seasoned adventurers equip themselves with various tools for different terrains, you, too, can be prepared for the emotional rollercoaster ride of puberty.

4

THE ABCS OF PERIODS

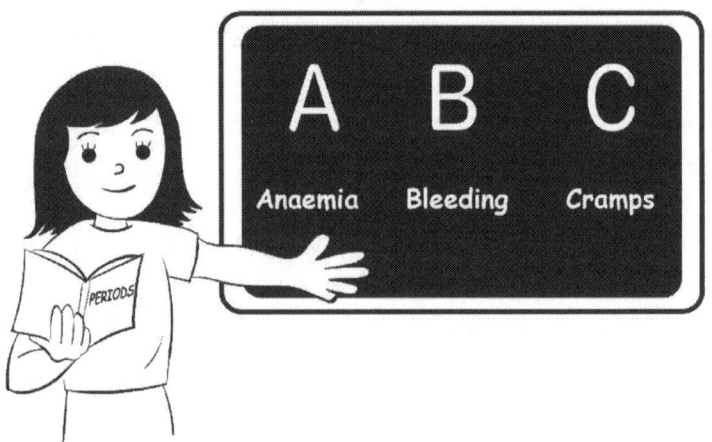

Hey there, curious kiddos! Have you ever heard grown-ups whisper about "that time of the month" or "Aunt Flo?" Maybe you've seen older sisters or moms using special pads or tampons. Well, it's all connected to something amazing called a period, and it's not a secret to be scared of! It's a superpower, and here's why:

A is for Amazing Body:

Every person with ovaries (the special egg-makers inside) has a super cool cycle happening. It's like a garden getting ready to plant a flower! Every month, the body builds a cozy nest inside, called the uterus, in case an egg gets fertilized and starts growing into a baby. But if no egg gets chosen, that nest doesn't need to stay anymore. So, the lining sheds and comes out as a little blood – that's your period!

B is for Brave Bodies:

Getting your period means your body is growing up and getting ready for the amazing possibility of creating life someday! It's a sign you're healthy and strong. Some people might feel cramps or mood swings during their period, but that's just your body adjusting. Everyone experiences it differently, and that's okay!

C is for Changing:

Periods usually last 3-7 days, and the blood might be light or heavy, like raindrops or a gentle stream. You might use pads, tampons, or period underwear to collect it – whichever feels most comfy for you! Remember, periods are natural and nothing to be embarrassed about. They happen to almost everyone with ovaries, and it's okay to talk about them openly and ask questions.

D is for Doctor Friend:

If you have any worries or questions about your period, don't hesitate to talk to your parents, a trusted adult, or even a doctor! They can explain things in more detail and help you feel prepared and confident.

Remember:

- Periods are a normal, healthy part of life for many people.
- Everyone's period is different, and that's okay!
- There's no shame in talking about periods, and asking questions is always a good idea.
- Your body is amazing, and your period is a superpower that shows you're growing and healthy!

Now that you know the ABCs of periods, let's meet some awesome Period Pals! These characters can answer your questions and help you confidently navigate your period journey:

Captain Calendar:

She keeps track of your cycle like a superhero sidekick! Mark your calendar with a fun symbol when your period starts so you're always prepared.

Mighty Mirror:

Check in with your body each day. Do you feel any cramps or mood changes? Mighty Mirror helps you recognize your unique period patterns.

Flow Fighters:

Pads, tampons, and period underwear are your trusty tools! Choose what feels most comfortable and secure for you. Remember, they're like shields protecting your clothes and keeping you feeling fresh.

Confidence Crew:

Talk to your friends, family, or healthcare professionals with questions or concerns. They're your cheerleaders, ready to support and empower you on your period journey.

You're not alone! Millions of people worldwide have periods, and many communities have fun traditions and celebrations related to them. Don't be afraid to ask for help if you need it. There are always people who care about you and want to support you. You will learn to embrace your period as a sign of your strength and health. It's part of what makes you unique and amazing!

Bonus Tip: Periods can sometimes feel messy, but remember, it's just your body doing its thing! Be kind to yourself, take care of your hygiene, and celebrate your superpower.

Now that you've met your squad and understand the basics, let's talk food! Just like any superhero needs the right fuel, your body craves certain nutrients during your period to feel its best. Think of these as Period Power Foods:

Hydration Hero:

Water is your best friend! Aim for plenty of glasses throughout the day to avoid dehydration, which can worsen cramps and headaches. Add some fun with fruit-infused water or herbal teas for extra flavor.

Fruit & Veggie Force:

Colorful fruits and veggies are packed with vitamins and minerals that help regulate your cycle and boost your mood. Think berries, leafy greens, oranges, and sweet potatoes – nature's candy for your body!

Whole Grain Warriors:

Brown rice, quinoa, and whole-wheat bread provide sustained energy and complex carbohydrates, helping you feel fuller for longer and avoid energy dips.

Omega-3 All-Stars:

Fatty fish like salmon, tuna, and sardines are champions of omega-3 fatty acids, known to reduce inflammation and ease cramps. Plus, they taste delicious!

Calcium Crusaders:

Dairy products like yogurt, milk, and cheese are powerhouses of calcium, which supports bone health and can help regulate muscle contractions, potentially reducing cramps. Plant-based options like leafy greens and fortified foods can also contribute.

Spice Squad:

Don't be afraid to sprinkle some magic with herbs and spices like ginger, turmeric, and cinnamon. These natural superheroes have anti-inflammatory properties and can help ease discomfort.

Remember to listen to your body! Are you craving a specific food? It might be your body sending signals for what it needs. Moderation is key. Enjoy treats in moderation, but don't forget to prioritize wholesome and nutritious choices. Experiment and find what works for you!

Everybody is unique, so discover the foods that make you feel your best during your period.

Why don't you keep a food diary to track how different foods affect your mood and energy levels during your cycle? This will help you make informed choices and personalize your Period Power Plate!

5
PIMPLES, ZITS, AND OTHER SKIN SURPRISES

Hey there, curious explorers of your amazing bodies! Ever wake up to a surprise volcano erupting on your face in the form of a pimple? Or maybe you've encountered mysterious bumps and patches that leave you scratching your head? Don't worry; these are just your body's way of communicating – it's a secret language waiting to be cracked!

These uninvited guests often appear when sebum (oil) gets trapped in your pores, creating a cozy home for bacteria. While they might seem like angry little bumps, remember, they're just your body trying to tell you something:

Hormonal Hello:

Puberty brings changes, and sometimes, hormones play a game of tug-of-war with your oil production, leading to breakouts.

Dirty Deeds:

Didn't wash your face after that sweaty sports game? Dirt and oil can team up to cause trouble.

Food Frenzy:

Certain foods might not agree with your skin. Listen to your body and see if any treats trigger breakouts.

Decoding Other Skin Surprises:

Red, Rough Patches:

Dry skin can sometimes act up and turn red and bumpy. Gentle moisturizers can be your superheroes in this case!

Itchy, Flaky Friends:

Dandruff on your scalp or eczema patches might signal your skin needs extra care. Talk to a grown-up for help finding the right solution.

Mysterious Marks:

Sometimes, bumps and marks can be allergies or insect bites. If they worry you, don't hesitate to ask a doctor or trusted adult.

Remember that your skin is unique, and what works for one person might not work for another. Experiment and find what soothes your skin best. Be gentle! Scrubbing too hard can irritate your skin and make things worse. Drink plenty of water, eat healthy foods, and get enough sleep – these are superpowers for healthy skin. Most importantly, don't be afraid to ask questions! There's no shame in wanting to understand your body and keep it happy.

Bonus Tip: Create a skincare routine that works for you. Cleanse gently, moisturize regularly, and use sunscreen daily (even on cloudy days!) to keep your skin healthy and glowing.

Pimples, zits, and other skin surprises – they may seem like uninvited guests at a party, but they're actually your body's way of communicating! Like a secret code, these bumps and patches hold clues about what's happening inside. Pimples and zits, those breakout buddies, often erupt when oil gets trapped and teams up with bacteria. This can happen when hormones play tug-of-war during puberty or when dirt and oil build up after forgetting to wash your face (oops!). Even certain foods can trigger these tiny volcanoes on your skin. But don't worry, there's no need to panic! Decoding these messages is easier than you think.

Dry skin might throw a tantrum with red, rough patches, while itchy, flaky friends like dandruff or eczema could signal your skin needs some TLC. Mysterious marks might be allergies or insect bites, but if they leave you puzzled, don't hesitate to ask a doctor or trusted adult for help. Remember, every skin is unique, like a snowflake! What works for one person's surprise might not work for yours. Experiment and find what soothes your skin best. Be gentle, too – scrubbing too hard is like yelling at your skin, and it won't make it happy.

The real superpowers for healthy skin? Water, nutritious food, and enough sleep! Think of them as potions and spells for your personal skin hero. And most importantly, never be afraid to ask questions! Understanding your body and keeping it happy is no secret – it's an adventure you're meant to enjoy. So, get ready to explore, experiment, and create a skincare routine that's just right for you. Cleanse gently, moisturize regularly, and don't forget the sunscreen – even on cloudy days! With a little care and understanding, your skin will be ready to face any surprise with confidence and glow.

Well, they're just part of the amazing journey called growing up! Your body is constantly changing, and your skin is the canvas that reflects these transformations. Just like a landscape shifts with seasons, your skin experiences different phases, each with its own unique features.

Let's explore some common chapters in this skin story:

The Puberty Plot Twist:

This exciting (and sometimes confusing) time can bring hormonal fluctuations that lead to breakouts. But don't despair! Gentle cleansing, targeted treatments, and a healthy lifestyle can help keep your skin balanced and glowing. Remember, you're not alone – almost everyone experiences this plot twist!

The Stressful Saga:

Feeling overwhelmed? It might show up on your skin as dryness, redness, or even breakouts. Take a deep breath, adventurer! Relaxation techniques like deep breathing, meditation, and spending time in nature can help your skin (and mind) find peace.

The Diet Dilemma:

What you put in your body affects what shows up on the outside. Sugary snacks and processed foods can trigger inflammation, while fruits, veggies, and whole grains provide nutrients that nourish your skin from within. Choose wisely, fuel your body well, and witness the transformation!

The Sleepless Scape:

Late nights spent studying or adventuring can leave your skin looking dull and tired. Aim for 9-12 hours of shut-eye each night to allow your skin to repair and regenerate. Think of it as a beauty sleep superpower!

Remember, every skin story is unique, and there's no one-size-fits-all solution. Embrace the journey, experiment with different approaches, and, most importantly, listen to your body. If a surprise persists or worries you, don't hesitate to seek guidance from a healthcare professional.

With a little understanding, self-care, and kindness, you can confidently navigate your skin's ever-changing landscape and celebrate its unique beauty. Remember, you're the author of your skin story, and every chapter holds the potential for growth, learning, and self-love. So go forth, explore, and write your own skin story – a tale of resilience, beauty, and ever-evolving wonder!

6

GROWING PAINS: NAVIGATING BODY CHANGES

Ever feel like your body is on a wild roller coaster ride? Growing up comes with many exciting changes, and sometimes, it can feel like your legs are having their party with aches and pains. Worry not; these are just "growing pains," little messages your body sends as it stretches and gets taller. But don't let them cramp your style! Here are some tips to understand and navigate these changes:

Imagine your bones like tiny construction crews building you taller! Sometimes, these crews work a little too hard, stretching your muscles too quickly, which can lead to those achy "growing pains," usually in your legs. They might come and go, especially at night, but remember, they're temporary and normal!

Growing pains might be annoying, but there are ways to soothe them. Gentle stretches before bed can help loosen up your muscles, and a warm bath with Epsom salts can work wonders. If the pain is strong, don't hesitate to ask your parents or a doctor for advice.

Growing up isn't just about height! Your body shape might change, and you might develop curves. This is all part of the amazing transformation into a young woman! Remember, everybody is unique and beautiful in their own way. Embrace your changes, and don't compare yourself to others. You're perfect just the way you are!

Just like superheroes need the right fuel, your growing body needs healthy food to keep it strong and happy. Think colorful fruits and veggies, whole grains, and lean protein. They'll give you the energy to explore, laugh, and confidently grow.

And never underestimate the power of sleep! Getting enough shut-eye (around 9-12 hours) helps your body repair and recharge, leaving you feeling refreshed and ready to tackle any adventure. Plus, it might even help keep those growing pains at bay!

Feeling confused or worried about body changes? Don't keep it bottled up! Talk to a trusted adult like your parents, a teacher, or even a doctor. They can answer your questions and offer support during this exciting, sometimes confusing, time.

Well, your body is like a superhero sending secret messages through these changes. Let's crack the code and understand what your body is trying to tell you:

The Hairy Situation:

Sprouts popping up in new places? Don't panic! It's your body signaling it's entering a new phase. Whether it's under your arms, on your legs, or even above your lips, remember it's totally normal (and hey, you can always ask your parents or an adult about hair removal options if you're curious!).

The Breast Buds Bloom:

Are you feeling little bumps under your chest? Those are your breast buds starting to develop! Think of them as tiny flower buds getting ready to bloom. Every girl's journey is unique, and their buds might blossom at different times. Embrace the changes, and remember, there's no such thing as "perfect" timing or size.

The Period Puzzle:

Have you ever heard whispers about "Aunt Flo" or "that time of the month"? It's all about periods! It means your body is preparing for the amazing possibility of creating life someday. Periods usually last 3-7 days, and you might experience some cramps, mood swings, or spotting – that's all part of the process. Don't be afraid to ask questions and learn more about this superpower your body possesses!

The Emotional Rollercoaster:

Sometimes, these changes can bring a whirlwind of emotions – feeling happy, excited, confused, or even frustrated is totally okay! Remember, your body is going through a lot, and your emotions are valid. Talk to a trusted friend, family member, or counselor if you need someone to listen and support you.

Now, it's time to celebrate the most important part of this journey: YOU! Your body is more than just bones, muscles, and skin; it's your amazing companion, your loyal friend, and a powerful machine capable of incredible things. Let's shift our focus from navigating changes to celebrating everything your body can do:

Think of your legs that carry you on adventures, your arms that hug loved ones, and your heart that pumps with kindness. Your body is strong, resilient, and capable of achieving great things. Celebrate its physical power whether you're dancing, playing sports, or simply exploring the world around you.

Taking care of your body is like nurturing a beautiful garden. Nourish it with healthy foods, move it with joyful activities, and give it the rest it needs. Remember, a healthy body is a happy body, and a happy body helps you shine from the inside out!

No two bodies are exactly alike, and that's what makes them all so incredibly beautiful! Celebrate your unique features, your favorite things about yourself, and the qualities that make you special. Don't compare yourself to others; embrace your individuality and let your inner beauty radiate.

Feeling confident in your skin is like wearing a superpower suit! But remember, true confidence comes from within. Be kind to yourself, practice positive self-talk, and surround yourself with people who support and appreciate you. When you feel good about yourself, it shows!

Did you know you can be a body positivity champion? Spread the message of self-love and acceptance to your friends, family, and community. Challenge unrealistic beauty standards, celebrate diversity, and remember that everyone deserves to feel good about their own amazing body.

This journey is all about YOU. Embrace the changes, celebrate your strengths, and nurture your body with love and care.

Remember: Every girl's experience is unique, and there's no one-size-fits-all approach to growing up. Embrace the changes, listen to your body, and celebrate its individuality. You are strong, capable, and amazing, just the way you are. So go forth, explore, and navigate your body talk journey with confidence and self-love!

And here's a table to help you with the journey so you don't freak out over any surprises…

Changes	Sources	Pains
Growing taller	Hormones	Growing pains in legs
Developing breasts	Hormones	Tenderness in breasts
Getting hair in new places	Hormones	None
Having your period	Hormones	Cramps, bloating
Mood swings	Hormones and brain chemistry	Irritability, sadness

7
LET'S TALK BRAS: FINDING THE PERFECT FIT

Remember that incredible body we've been celebrating? Bras are awesome tools that support your growing breasts and keep things comfy during all your adventures. But with so many sizes, styles, and straps, finding the perfect fit can feel like deciphering a secret code. Worry not, adventurers! This guide will help you navigate the bra-niverse and discover your ideal match.

Everybody develops at their own pace, so there's no set age to start wearing a bra. It's all about when you start feeling changes in your chest area – tenderness, slight bumps, or the need for extra support. If you find yourself adjusting your shirt a lot or feeling uncomfortable, a bra might be your new best friend!

Breaking Down the Basics:

First, let's talk sizing. Bras come in two main parts: the band and the cups. The band goes around your back, and the cups cover your breasts. Both should fit snugly but comfortably without digging in or feeling loose.

The Measuring Mission:

To find your band size, measure yourself directly under your breasts, keeping the measuring tape snug but not tight. Add 3 inches to your measurement for your starting band size. For example, if your measurement is 30 inches, your starting band size would be 33.

Next, measure the fullest part of your bust (around your nipples), keeping the tape level. Subtract your band size from your bust measurement to find your cup size. Here's the breakdown:

A difference of 1 inch = A cup

A difference of 2 inches = B cup

A difference of 3 inches = C cup

A difference of 4 inches = D cup

This is just a starting point, so don't worry if your measurements don't fall perfectly into this chart. Everyone's unique!

The Fitting Fun:

Now comes the fun part – trying on bras! Head to a store with knowledgeable staff who can guide you through the process. Tell them your measurements and any concerns you have. Don't be shy about asking questions and trying on different styles and sizes until you find one that feels just right.

Signs of a Perfect Fit:

- The band sits comfortably around your back without digging in or riding up.
- The cups fully enclose your breasts without spilling over or gapping.
- The straps stay put without digging into your shoulders.
- You can move freely and comfortably without feeling restricted.
- It's normal to try on several bras before finding the perfect fit.
- Your size might change as your body continues to develop.
- Comfort is key! Don't wear a bra that hurts or feels uncomfortable.

There are different types of bras for different activities, like sports bras for high-impact activities and everyday bras for comfort. Talk to your parents, guardians, or trusted adults if you have any questions or concerns.

Conquered the measuring mission and found your starting size? Awesome! But the bra-niverse holds more than just basic styles. Buckle up, adventurers, because we're diving into different bra types for all your activities!

Sports Star:

Whether you're hitting the court, field, or gym, a supportive sports bra is your champion! Look for thicker straps, wider bands, and moisture-wicking fabrics to keep you comfy and focused on your game.

Everyday Explorer:

Need a bra for casual hangouts, school days, or just chilling at home? Comfort is key! Choose soft, breathable fabrics like cotton or microfiber. Consider wireless styles for extra freedom or opt for lightly padded options for a touch of shaping.

Growing & Changing: Remember, your body continues to develop, so don't be surprised if your perfect fit changes over time. Re-measure every few months, especially during growth spurts, to ensure your bra still offers the proper support.

Beyond the Fit: Feeling self-conscious about wearing a bra? It's totally normal! Talk to your friends, family, or a trusted adult about your feelings. Remember, bras are tools to help you feel comfortable and confident, not something to be ashamed of.

Celebrate Your Body:

No matter your size or shape, your body is amazing! Wearing a bra is a way to show yourself love and care. Embrace your unique shape and rock that bra with confidence!

This bra adventure is about finding what makes you feel good and empowered. Experiment, ask questions, and don't hesitate to ask for help. Remember, the perfect bra is the one that makes you feel like the incredible adventurer you are, ready to conquer anything with comfort and confidence! So go forth, explore, and embrace the fun of finding your perfect fit!

8
HAIR TODAY, GONE TOMORROW: A GUIDE TO BODY HAIR

Remember that incredible body we've been celebrating? Well, guess what? Hair might be popping up in new places, and that's totally normal! But navigating this new terrain can feel like deciphering a jungle code. Worry not, adventurers, because this guide will help you confidently understand, manage, and even embrace your body hair journey.

As you grow up, your body goes through some really cool changes, and one of them is getting some new hair in different places. It's like a magical transformation; the best part is that it's totally normal!

Now, let's talk about the two main types of body hair. First up, we have Vellus Hair. This is the soft and fine hair that's been with you since the day you were born. During puberty, it might start to show up a bit more, but don't worry, it's just your body doing its thing.

Next, meet Terminal Hair. This is the thicker, coarser hair that appears in places like your underarms, legs, and genital area. It's like a little sign that your body is growing up and becoming more adult-like. Isn't that fascinating?

Everyone's journey is different so that you might notice these changes at your own unique pace. And you know what? That's super cool! You're becoming the incredible person you're meant to be.

Hair growth is powered by hormones, and during puberty, these little messengers start sending signals to different parts of your body, telling them to sprout some fuzz. Your legs, underarms, and even areas around your bikini line might suddenly become mini-jungles. Remember, this is all part of the amazing transformation your body is going through!

The Big Question is: "To Remove or Not to Remove?"

The decision of whether to remove body hair is entirely yours! There's no right or wrong answer, and what works for one person might not be the best fit for another. Consider these factors:

- **Comfort:** Does the hair bother you physically or make you feel self-conscious?
- **Lifestyle:** Do you prefer a smoother feel for certain activities like sports or wearing specific clothing?

- **Maintenance:** Different removal methods require varying levels of time, effort, and cost.
- **Personal Preference:** Ultimately, it's about what makes you feel most comfortable and confident in your own skin!

The timing of body hair growth varies for everyone. Some may notice it early in puberty, while others might experience it later. Remember, there's no rush or specific schedule for these changes. It's all part of the unique and incredible journey your body is on.

1. Understanding Body Hair Growth:

Puberty, the magical journey of becoming a teenager, brings about various changes, including the appearance of body hair. It's crucial to understand that these changes are entirely normal and a natural part of growing up. Body hair growth occurs due to the increase in hormones, and each person's experience is unique.

2. Hygiene is Key:

Maintaining good hygiene becomes essential as you embark on this journey. Regular bathing and cleansing not only keep you feeling fresh but also contribute to the health of your skin and hair follicles. Using a mild soap or body wash is crucial to prevent irritation and maintain the natural balance of your skin.

3. Choosing Hair Removal Methods:

Sometimes, you might want to remove or manage body hair, and that's absolutely okay. Various methods are available, each with its own pros and cons.

- **Shaving:** This is a common and quick method. However, hair grows back relatively quickly, and there's a risk of nicks or irritation.

- **Waxing:** This method provides longer-lasting results as it removes hair from the root. However, it can be a bit uncomfortable, especially for beginners.
- **Hair Removal Creams:** These creams dissolve the hair, providing a painless option. It's essential to follow instructions carefully to avoid skin irritation.

The key is to choose a method that suits your preferences and comfort level. What works for one person may not be the best for another, so it's all about finding what makes you feel good.

4. Be Patient:

Patience is your best friend during puberty. Body hair growth is a gradual process, and the timing varies for everyone. If you're eagerly waiting for changes to appear, remember that your body is unique, and development happens at its own pace. Comparing yourself to others isn't necessary because everyone's journey is different.

5. Building Body Positivity:

Embracing body hair is an integral part of building body positivity. Your body is undergoing incredible transformations, and every stage is beautiful in its way. Celebrate the uniqueness of your body and appreciate the journey it's taking you on.

6. Open Communication:

Having questions or concerns about body hair is normal. If you're unsure or curious, don't hesitate to talk to a trusted adult, like a parent, guardian, or healthcare professional. They can provide guidance, answer your questions, and ensure you feel comfortable and informed about these natural changes.

7. Respecting Individual Choices:

Remember, managing or removing body hair is a personal choice. Some people prefer to embrace their natural state, while others may choose grooming methods. Whatever you decide, it's essential to respect your own choices and the choices of others. Everyone's journey is unique, and there's no right or wrong way to navigate it.

8. Caring for Your Skin:

Whether you decide to keep or remove body hair, caring for your skin is crucial. Use moisturizers or lotions to keep your skin hydrated, especially after hair removal. This helps prevent dryness and irritation, ensuring your skin stays healthy and comfortable.

9. Growing Into Confidence:

Puberty is not just about physical changes; it's also a time of self-discovery and building confidence. Embrace the changes, be kind to yourself, and know that every step of this journey is an opportunity to grow into the confident and amazing person you're destined to be.

10. Seeking Support and Guidance:

If you ever feel overwhelmed or have questions, seek support and guidance from those you trust. Parents, guardians, or healthcare professionals are there to provide assistance and ensure you have the information you need to navigate this exciting phase of your life.

Remember, you're not alone in this journey, and every aspect of your body's transformation is part of the incredible adventure of growing up.

9
THE MONTHLY VISITOR: DEALING WITH PERIODS

Have you ever heard hushed whispers about "Aunt Flo" or "that time of the month?" Ever wondered what everyone's giggling about? Well, adventurer, it's time to demystify the secret code! This chapter dives into the world of periods – a natural part of your amazing body's journey.

But don't worry, we're not just talking about cramps and pads. We'll navigate the emotional swings, unravel the physical changes, and explore the superpowers that come with this monthly visitor. Get ready to crack the code, celebrate your incredible body, and embrace the amazing woman you're becoming!

Remember, every girl's experience is unique, and there's no one-size-fits-all guide. This chapter is here to empower you with knowledge, answer your questions, and provide a safe space to confidently explore your changing body. So, buckle up, adventurer, and prepare to unlock the secrets of the monthly visitor – a powerful symbol of your transformation and womanhood!

We'll cover everything from understanding the "why" behind periods to managing the practicalities. Don't be afraid to ask questions, explore different solutions, and celebrate your unique cycle. Remember, periods are a natural part of life, and having them means your body is working its magic! You've got this, and this chapter is your trusty guide on this exciting journey of self-discovery and empowerment.

Ever wondered why grown-ups sometimes whisper about "that time of the month"? It's all about a secret power your body has – periods! These aren't scary monsters hiding in your tummy, but a cool sign that your body is growing and getting ready for amazing things.

Imagine your body like a super cool garden. Every month, it builds a cozy nest, just in case a tiny seed called an egg wants to grow there and become a baby someday. But if that doesn't happen, your body cleans up the nest and starts building a new one again. That's what a period is – a way of getting ready for next month's adventure!

Think of tiny messengers called hormones like helpers in this garden. They zoom around telling your body what to do, and sometimes they might make you feel a little moody or have tummy cramps. But don't worry, that's just them working hard to keep your garden healthy and ready!

Having periods every month is like showing off your superpower! It means your body is working just the way it should, growing strong and amazing. And guess what? You're not alone in this! Millions of girls and women worldwide experience periods, and they can answer all your questions and share tips to make things easier.

So next time you hear hushed whispers about periods, remember, it's not something to be scared of! It's a sign of your incredible body doing its magic. This chapter is your guide to unlocking the secrets of periods, understanding how they work, and celebrating your body's amazing power.

Now we get the serious talk: How can we be prepared?

First things first, knowledge is power! Talk to your parents, older sister, or doctor about periods. Ask them all your questions, no matter how small or silly they might seem. The more you know, the more prepared and confident you'll feel.

Next, explore your options! Pads, tampons, and period panties are like different tools for different situations. Talk to your trusted adult about trying each one to see what feels most comfortable for you. Remember, there's no right or wrong choice – it's all about what makes you feel good!

Don't be afraid to stock up! Having pads, tampons, or your chosen supplies on hand means you'll never be caught off guard. Keep a stash in your backpack, locker, or even a small pouch in your purse – wherever you feel most comfortable.

Pack an "emergency kit" with essentials like wipes, pain relievers, and maybe even a change of clothes (just in case!). Knowing you have everything you need will help you relax and confidently handle any situation.

Remember, periods are natural, and your body might send some warning signs before they arrive. Feeling a little cramping, extra tired, or even having mood swings are all totally normal. Knowing these "period signals" can help you prepare and adjust your day.

Talk to your friends! Chances are, they've already started their periods or are about to, and sharing experiences can be super helpful. You can support each other, swap tips, and remind each other that you're not alone in this.

Lastly, remember, be kind to yourself! Periods are a new part of your journey, and it might take some time to adjust. Don't get discouraged if things feel messy or confusing at first. Embrace the learning process, celebrate your body's amazing changes, and remember, you've got this!

So, get ready, adventurers! With a little planning and knowledge, you'll be a period prep pro, ready to conquer every cycle with confidence and a smile.

Now, think of yourself as a game player. You have made a step, and now you are a step closer to being the ultimate pro. You've prepped like a pro, and now your amazing body has entered a new cycle. But don't worry; even with Aunt Flo visiting, you can conquer anything with the right knowledge and tools. Let's dive into the ABCs of managing your period with confidence:

cramps. But don't worry, that's just them working hard to keep your garden healthy and ready!

Having periods every month is like showing off your superpower! It means your body is working just the way it should, growing strong and amazing. And guess what? You're not alone in this! Millions of girls and women worldwide experience periods, and they can answer all your questions and share tips to make things easier.

So next time you hear hushed whispers about periods, remember, it's not something to be scared of! It's a sign of your incredible body doing its magic. This chapter is your guide to unlocking the secrets of periods, understanding how they work, and celebrating your body's amazing power.

Now we get the serious talk: How can we be prepared?

First things first, knowledge is power! Talk to your parents, older sister, or doctor about periods. Ask them all your questions, no matter how small or silly they might seem. The more you know, the more prepared and confident you'll feel.

Next, explore your options! Pads, tampons, and period panties are like different tools for different situations. Talk to your trusted adult about trying each one to see what feels most comfortable for you. Remember, there's no right or wrong choice – it's all about what makes you feel good!

Don't be afraid to stock up! Having pads, tampons, or your chosen supplies on hand means you'll never be caught off guard. Keep a stash in your backpack, locker, or even a small pouch in your purse – wherever you feel most comfortable.

Pack an "emergency kit" with essentials like wipes, pain relievers, and maybe even a change of clothes (just in case!). Knowing you have everything you need will help you relax and confidently handle any situation.

Remember, periods are natural, and your body might send some warning signs before they arrive. Feeling a little cramping, extra tired, or even having mood swings are all totally normal. Knowing these "period signals" can help you prepare and adjust your day.

Talk to your friends! Chances are, they've already started their periods or are about to, and sharing experiences can be super helpful. You can support each other, swap tips, and remind each other that you're not alone in this.

Lastly, remember, be kind to yourself! Periods are a new part of your journey, and it might take some time to adjust. Don't get discouraged if things feel messy or confusing at first. Embrace the learning process, celebrate your body's amazing changes, and remember, you've got this!

So, get ready, adventurers! With a little planning and knowledge, you'll be a period prep pro, ready to conquer every cycle with confidence and a smile.

Now, think of yourself as a game player. You have made a step, and now you are a step closer to being the ultimate pro. You've prepped like a pro, and now your amazing body has entered a new cycle. But don't worry; even with Aunt Flo visiting, you can conquer anything with the right knowledge and tools. Let's dive into the ABCs of managing your period with confidence:

A is for Awareness: Remember those "period signals" we talked about? Pay attention to your body! Cramps, bloating, mood swings, or fatigue can be early signs. This awareness helps you prepare and adjust your plans if needed.

B is for Being Prepared: Keep your handy "emergency kit" close by. Pack extra pads, tampons, wipes, pain relievers, and even a change of clothes for unexpected leaks. Feeling prepared reduces stress and empowers you to handle anything.

C is for Comfort is Key: Find what works best for you! Experiment with different pad sizes, tampon absorbencies, or period panties. Choose soft, breathable materials that feel comfortable against your skin.

D is for Don't Panic: It's normal to initially feel nervous or confused. Talk to your parents, friends, or a doctor if you have questions or concerns. They can offer support and guidance.

E is for Easy Does It: Periods can make you feel tired, so listen to your body. Rest when you need to, and don't be afraid to ask for help with chores or schoolwork. Take breaks, do relaxing activities, and prioritize your well-being.

F is for Flow with Your Feelings: Mood swings are common during periods. Talk to friends or family if you feel cranky or emotional. Remember, it's temporary, and expressing yourself can help you feel better.

G is for Groove on: Don't let your period stop you from living your life! You can still exercise, participate in activities, and have fun. Just adjust the intensity or choose things you enjoy doing even when you don't feel your best.

H is for Hydration Hero: Drink plenty of water to stay hydrated and fight bloating. Avoid sugary drinks that can make cramps worse.

I is for Information is Power: Keep learning about periods! Read books articles or talk to trusted adults. The more you know, the more comfortable and confident you'll feel.

J is for Join the Conversation: Don't feel ashamed to talk about periods! Share experiences with friends and family, or even join online communities. Remember, you're not alone, and talking openly can help break down stigma.

K is for Kindness to Yourself: Be patient and understanding with your body. Periods are a natural part of being a girl; everyone experiences them differently. Celebrate your strength and resilience!

L is for Listen to Your Body: Each period is unique. Sometimes you might need more rest or less activity. Pay attention to how you feel and adjust your routine accordingly.

M is for Mindfulness Matters: Stress can make cramps worse. Practice relaxation techniques like deep breathing or meditation to manage stress and feel calmer.

N is for No Shame in the Name: Periods are nothing to be ashamed of! They're a sign of your body's amazing capabilities. Hold your head high and embrace this natural part of who you are.

O is for Open Communication: If you experience pain, heavy bleeding, or irregular cycles, talk to your doctor. They can provide support and address any concerns you might have.

P is for Period Power: Remember, periods are a sign of your body's incredible strength and potential. Celebrate your unique cycle and embrace the amazing woman you are becoming!

This alphabet is just a starting point. As you navigate your period journey, discover new tips, adjust routines, and build your own confidence toolkit. Remember, you've got this, adventurer! Periods are a natural part of your life, and you have the power to manage them with knowledge, self-care, and a positive attitude. Go forth and flow confidently, knowing you are strong, capable, and absolutely incredible!

10

CRACKING THE CODE OF CRAMPS

#_CRAMPS

R emember how we explored the amazing journey of periods? Well, sometimes, this journey comes with a bit of a bumpy road – in the form of cramps! Don't worry; these tummy troubles don't have to stop you from conquering your day. We're here to crack the code of cramps, understand why they happen, and equip you with tools to manage them like a superhero!

Think of your uterus like a super cool muscle that gets ready to welcome a tiny seed someday. During your period, this muscle contracts to shed its lining, and sometimes, these contractions can cause those uncomfortable cramps you feel. Remember, it's your body doing its thing, but that doesn't mean you have to suffer!

Every girl experiences cramps differently – some might feel mild twinges, while others might have stronger sensations. Knowing your "cramp code" is the first step to managing them effectively. Pay attention to the intensity, duration, and any patterns you notice. This information will help you choose the right strategies.

There's no magic spell to banish cramps entirely, but there are plenty of ways to fight back! Gentle movement like walking, yoga, or stretching can help ease muscle tension. A warm bath or a heating pad on your tummy can work wonders, too. Don't underestimate the power of a comfy, cozy blanket and a cup of warm tea!

Talking to your parents, trusted adults or even a doctor can be super helpful. They can share tips based on their own experiences and offer guidance specific to your needs. Remember, you're not alone in this, and asking for help is a sign of strength, not weakness.

Sometimes, over-the-counter pain relievers can be a lifesaver. Talk to your doctor or pharmacist to find the right option for you, and always follow the dosage instructions carefully. Remember, prevention is key! Staying hydrated, eating healthy foods, and getting enough sleep can all help reduce cramps before they even start.

This chapter is your guide to becoming a cramp-conquering champion! We'll explore different strategies, answer your questions, and empower you to navigate this part of your period journey with confidence. Remember, you are strong, capable, and ready to tackle any challenge, even those pesky belly blahs! So, get ready to unlock the secrets of cramps and conquer your cycle with a smile.

So, What Do You Do to Get Rid of Cramps?

Ugh, cramps! Those unwelcome visitors can definitely take the shine off your day. But don't worry, adventurer, you're not powerless! Here are some strategies to help you manage cramps and keep your adventure spirit soaring:

Movement is Magic:

Gentle movement can be your best friend when it comes to cramps. Try some light stretches, take a walk around the block, or even do some yoga poses specifically designed for period relief. Moving your body helps ease muscle tension and get your blood flowing, both of which can help soothe those tummy troubles.

Heat Up the Hero:

Heat is a pain reliever's superpower! Whether it's a warm bath, a heating pad on your tummy, or even a hot water bottle wrapped in a towel, applying heat can work wonders. The warmth relaxes your muscles and promotes blood flow, easing those crampy sensations.

Cozy Comfort:

Sometimes, the best medicine is simply taking it easy. Curl up on the couch with a cozy blanket, read a good book, or watch your favorite movie. Taking time to relax and de-stress can do wonders for both your body and mind, helping your cramps become less bothersome.

Hydration Heroics:

Dehydration can actually worsen cramps! Make sure you drink plenty of water throughout the day, especially when feeling crampy. Water helps flush out toxins and keeps your body functioning smoothly, which can help reduce discomfort.

Food Choices Make a Difference:

What you eat can impact your cramps! Try to avoid sugary drinks and processed foods, which can contribute to inflammation and worsen pain. Instead, focus on fruits, vegetables, and whole grains, which are packed with nutrients that can help reduce inflammation and boost your overall well-being.

Herbal Helpers:

Talk to your parents or doctor about trying natural remedies like ginger tea or turmeric, which have anti-inflammatory properties and might offer some relief. Remember, though, that everyone reacts differently, so start with small amounts and see how your body feels.

Pain Relief Partners:

If cramps are really getting in the way, over-the-counter pain relievers like ibuprofen or acetaminophen can be helpful. Always talk to your parents or doctor first to choose the right medication and dosage for you and remember to follow the instructions carefully.

Don't Suffer in Silence:

Remember, you're not alone! Talk to your friends, family, or even a doctor if you're struggling with cramps. They can offer support, share their own experiences, and help you find strategies that work best for you.

These are just a few starting points... Experiment with different approaches, find what works best for you, and remember, knowledge is power! The more you understand about cramps and your own body, the better equipped you'll be to manage them and keep living your incredible life to the fullest.

Outsmarting Cramps with Fun & Laughter!

We know they can bring your sunshine down, but don't worry, adventurer! Even while your tummy might be throwing a mini tantrum, there are tons of awesome distractions to whisk you away to a land of fun and forgetfulness. Let's outsmart those cramps with laughter, creativity, and some seriously cool activities!

Funny Fiesta:

Laughter is the best medicine, even for cramps! Put on your favorite comedy show, watch silly animal videos, or read a hilarious book. Laughter boosts your mood and can help relax your muscles, making those cramps feel less powerful.

Creative Corner:

Unleash your inner artist! Draw, paint, sculpt, write a story, or even design your own fashion line. Getting lost in a creative project can take your mind off the discomfort and allow you to express yourself in a fun and meaningful way.

Music Magic:

Put on your headphones and blast your favorite tunes! Dance around your room, sing at the top of your lungs, or create your own silly song about conquering cramps. Music has a powerful way of changing your mood and can be a great source of comfort and energy.

Cozy Movie Marathon:

Snuggle up under a blanket with some popcorn and your favorite movies. Whether it's a classic animated film, a heartwarming comedy, or an action-packed adventure, getting lost in a good story can transport you to another world and help you forget about your troubles.

Board Game Bonanza:

Gather your friends or family for a board game bonanza! From classics like Monopoly and Scrabble to silly party games like Charades and Pictionary, laughter and friendly competition can be the perfect antidote to cramping woes.

Puzzles & Challenges:

Put your brain to the test with challenging puzzles, crosswords, or logic games. Focusing on problem-solving can take your mind off the discomfort and give you a sense of accomplishment when you complete a tricky task.

DIY Delights:

Get crafty and create something awesome! From decorating your room to making origami animals, there are endless DIY projects that are both fun and engaging. Plus, you'll have something cool to show off at the end!

Nature Nurturing:

Take a walk in the park, breathe in the fresh air, and listen to the sounds of nature. Immersing yourself in nature can be incredibly calming and restorative, helping you feel more relaxed and connected to the world around you.

Bubble Bath Bliss:

Fill the tub with warm water, drop in some fun bath bombs or bubbles, and create your own relaxing spa experience. Add some calming music and a good book, and you've got the perfect recipe for pampering and forgetting about those pesky cramps.

Remember, adventurer, you're not alone in this! Talk to your friends, family, or even a doctor if you're feeling overwhelmed. But most importantly, don't let cramps stop you from having fun and enjoying your life.

11

PMS SOS: TAMING THE MONTHLY BEAST

We've explored periods, cramps, and all the amazing things your body can do. But sometimes, there's another visitor who can show up – PMS, the Premenstrual Syndrome. Don't worry, adventurer, this "beast" might seem scary, but with knowledge and self-care, you can tame it and keep conquering your days!

Think of PMS like a roller coaster of emotions and physical changes that happen before your period. Yes, there might be mood swings, fatigue, or even breakouts, but remember, it's all temporary and perfectly normal. This chapter is your guide to understanding PMS, learning how to manage its ups and downs, and, most importantly, celebrating your amazing body even when it throws you a curveball.

We'll explore the different PMS symptoms, debunk some myths, and equip you with strategies to feel your best. You'll discover healthy foods, relaxation techniques, and even fun activities to help you confidently navigate these pre-period changes. Remember, every girl experience PMS differently, so there's no one-size-fits-all answer. This chapter is here to empower you to listen to your body, find what works for you, and embrace the unique rhythm of your cycle.

With periods and superpowers and all that cool stuff? Well, sometimes, before the period party arrives, there's this guest on the scene called PMS, which stands for Pre-Menstrual Syndrome (say that ten times fast!). Now, PMS might sound like a scary monster hiding under your bed, but don't worry; it's more like a roller coaster ride of emotions and physical changes.

Think of your body as a super cool amusement park. Every month, it gets ready for this amazing event called ovulation (like a big carnival!), and sometimes, before the carnival opens, the ride operators (hormones) get a little excited, and things get a bit... bumpy. That's PMS!

So, what does this rollercoaster ride feel like? Well, everyone experiences it differently, but you might feel things like…

1. **Mood swings**: One minute, you're laughing like a hyena; the next minute, you might feel like crying over a spilled juice box. It's okay; those rollercoaster cars love to zoom up and down!

2. **Fatigue:** Feeling extra tired? The ride operators are probably working overtime, making you want to take a nap in the cotton candy stand (your cozy bed!).

3. **Cravings**: Feeling like you could eat an entire pizza (and maybe some fries on the side)? It's like your taste buds are on a sugar rush, waiting for all the carnival treats!

4. **Breakouts**: Uh oh, little spots might pop up like popcorn at the concession stand. Don't worry; they're temporary party guests that will fade away soon.

Remember, all these changes are totally normal and happen because your amazing body is doing its thing! But like on a rollercoaster, you might sometimes want to adjust your ride experience. Here are some fun tips:

Snack Smart:

Instead of grabbing greasy treats, choose fruits, veggies, and whole grains – they're like healthy rollercoaster fuel!

Move Your Body:

Exercise is like a stress-busting machine! A walk, a dance party, or even some jumping jacks can help smooth out those bumpy rides.

Chill Out Zone:

Are you feeling overwhelmed? Take some deep breaths, read a book, or do something calming, like taking a warm bath – it's like hitting the "relaxation station" on the ride!

Talk it Out:

Are you feeling confused or frustrated? Chat with your parents, friends, or a trusted adult – they can be your rollercoaster buddies and offer support!

Remember, adventurer, PMS is just a part of your incredible journey. With a little understanding, self-care, and a positive attitude, you can navigate those pre-period ups and downs like a pro!

Think of PMS like a roller coaster of emotions and physical changes that happen before your period. Yes, there might be mood swings, fatigue, or even breakouts, but remember, it's all temporary and perfectly normal. To help you navigate this pre-period rollercoaster with confidence, we've put together a fun table with all the info you need!

Symptom	PMS Party Crasher?	Battle Buddy Strategies	When to Expect It?
Mood Swings	Feeling like you're riding an emotional rollercoaster?	Chill Out Zone: Take deep breaths, do calming activities like yoga or meditation, and talk to a friend or family member.	1-2 weeks before your period
Fatigue	Feeling like you could nap through a rock concert?	Fuel Up Smart: Choose healthy snacks like fruits, veggies, and whole grains for sustained energy.	1-2 weeks before your period
Cravings	Suddenly craving everything from pizza to pickles?	Snack Attack Strategy: Opt for healthier alternatives like fruit with yogurt or veggie sticks with hummus.	1-2 weeks before your period

Breakouts	Feeling like your face is having a party of uninvited pimples?	Skincare Savior: Stick to your regular skincare routine and avoid touching your face too much.	1-2 weeks before your period
Bloating	Feeling like your tummy is a bouncy castle?	Hydration Hero: Drink plenty of water and avoid salty foods that worsen bloating.	1 week before your period
Headaches	Feeling like your head is having a mini earthquake?	Headache Hero: Get enough sleep, stay hydrated, and try relaxation techniques like gentle stretches.	1-2 weeks before your period

This table is a starting point to help you identify symptoms and find strategies that work best for you. Don't hesitate to talk to your parents, friends, or doctor if you have questions or concerns. With knowledge, self-care, and a positive attitude, you can conquer the PMS rollercoaster and embrace your amazing body every step of the way.

12

THE SCIENCE BEHIND MENSTRUATION

Have you ever wondered why your body embarks on this monthly adventure called menstruation? It's more than just blood and cramps – it's a fascinating biological dance driven by tiny messengers and powerful hormones! Buckle up, adventurers, as we delve into the science behind periods and unlock the secrets of this incredible process.

Imagine your body as a magnificent garden, nurturing a tiny seed called an egg, hoping it might one day grow into a baby. Every month, your body prepares a cozy nest for this seed. It builds a soft lining in your uterus, rich in nutrients, ready to support the egg if it gets fertilized. But if fertilization doesn't happen, that lining doesn't get used. That's when things get interesting!

Tiny chemical messengers called hormones, like the master gardeners of your body, play a crucial role. One hormone, estrogen, helps build the cozy lining in your uterus. Another, progesterone, helps keep it ready for the egg. But if no fertilization occurs, these hormone levels drop like falling leaves.

With the hormone shift, the lining in your uterus starts to break down. Think of it like gently composting fallen leaves to nourish the soil for the next cycle. This breakdown process causes some of the lining to leave your body through your vagina – that's your period!

And guess what? This blood isn't just "waste." It's a mix of tissue, blood cells, and other materials no longer needed. So, having a period is your body's way of cleaning the house and getting ready for the next month's potential adventure.

Now, the science gets even cooler! Did you know the average menstrual cycle lasts about 28 days? But don't worry if yours is shorter or longer – everyone's body has its own unique rhythm. And while some girls might experience mild cramps or mood swings, others won't. It's all perfectly normal!

Here are some bonus science facts to impress your friends:

- The fluid released during your period isn't exactly the same as blood. It has fewer blood cells and more water.

- The thickness and amount of your period can vary from month to month and throughout your life.

- Your body starts preparing for its first period years before it actually arrives – during puberty.

The curtain has been lifted on the fascinating science behind menstruation. It's not just a physical experience but a complex symphony of hormones, cellular processes, and biological adaptations. Your body is a marvel of engineering, and your period is a testament to its incredible ability to prepare for life, adapt to change, and renew itself month after month.

But remember, science isn't the whole story. There's also the cultural aspect, the emotional side, and each individual's unique experiences. Periods can be messy, inconvenient, and sometimes even uncomfortable. But they also symbolize strength, resilience, and the power of creation within you.

Embracing both the science and the personal experience of menstruation is key to developing a healthy and positive relationship with your body. Don't be afraid to ask questions, talk to trusted adults, and explore different perspectives. Remember, knowledge is power, and understanding your cycle empowers you to make informed choices, manage any challenges, and celebrate the incredible journey your body embarks on each month.

Getting Ready?

You learned about the science, the emotions, and the incredible power your body holds. But what if that first period is still far away, or maybe just around the corner? Don't worry, adventurer, we've got you covered! Here's how to prepare for your big debut with confidence and excitement:

Knowledge is Power:

Read Up: Books, articles, and websites can be excellent resources for understanding periods. Ask your parents, librarian, or doctor for recommendations.

Talk it Out: Chat with your parents, older sister, or a trusted adult about their experiences. They can answer your questions and offer support.

Join the Club!: Online communities and support groups can connect you with girls going through the same thing, helping you feel less alone.

Be Prepared:

Stock Up: Keep pads, tampons, or period panties on hand, even if you think your period is far away. Different options exist, so explore and find what feels most comfortable for you.

Pack an Emergency Kit: Stash pads, wipes, pain relievers, and even a change of clothes in your backpack or locker for unexpected leaks.

Know the Signs: Some girls experience cramps, mood swings, or fatigue before their period. Pay attention to your body's signals to be prepared.

Stay Positive:

Embrace the Change: Periods are a natural part of life, not something to be embarrassed about. Celebrate your body's amazing power to create and nurture!

Don't Panic: If you experience your first period unexpectedly, remember it's totally normal. Ask for help from a trusted adult, and they'll guide you through it.

Self-care is Key: Be kind to yourself! Get enough sleep, eat healthy foods, and try relaxation techniques like deep breathing or meditation to manage any discomfort.

Remember, every girl is different:

The Timing is Unique: Your first period can arrive anytime between ages 8 and 13. Don't compare yourself to others – your body has its own timeline.

The Experience Varies: Some girls have light periods, while others have heavier ones. Cramps and mood swings can also vary in intensity. It's all perfectly normal!

Ask for Help, Always: If you have questions, concerns, or experience anything unusual, don't hesitate to talk to your parents, doctor, or another trusted adult. They're there to support you every step of the way.

13

PUBERTY POWER: DISCOVERING YOUR STRENGTH

Puberty

Remember how we explored the amazing magic of periods? It's just one incredible part of a bigger adventure called puberty – a time of transformation, growth, and discovering thesuperhero powers within you! Don't worry, adventurer, this might sound overwhelming, but it's actually an exciting journey of self-discovery, filled with wonder and potential.

Think of puberty like your body pressing the "upgrade" button. Just like your favorite video game character, you're leveling up, gaining new abilities, and unlocking exciting features. It might come with some temporary glitches – mood swings, growth spurts, maybe even the occasional zit – but those are just side effects of your amazing transformation.

This chapter is your guide to navigating puberty like a pro! We'll explore the physical changes you might experience, from new curves to deeper voices, and empower you to understand and celebrate them. We'll delve into the emotional rollercoaster that can come with fluctuating hormones, teaching you tools to manage mood swings and embrace your unique feelings.

But puberty isn't just about changes on the outside – it's also a time of incredible internal growth. You'll develop new interests, discover hidden talents, and start forming your own opinions and beliefs. It's like unlocking new skills and powers in your personality, making you stronger, more confident, and ready to conquer any challenge.

Along the way, you might face new situations and emotions. Don't worry, you're not alone! This chapter will be your trusted companion, offering advice, support, and resources to help you navigate everything from body image struggles to peer pressure.

Remember, there's no one "right" way to experience puberty – it's your own unique journey.

Here's a deeper dive into the physical and emotional changes you might encounter on your amazing journey:

Let's break down all the changes you can go through physically.

Growth spurts:

Imagine waking up one morning and feeling like your clothes shrunk in the wash! That's the magic of growth spurts. Your bones and muscles are rapidly growing, making you taller and stronger. Embrace this change – your body is building a strong foundation for your future. Remember, even though your clothes might feel a little snug, you're becoming the incredible and powerful person you were meant to be!

Body changes:

As your body matures, your shape will naturally start to change. You might develop new curves, wider hips, or broader shoulders. These changes are unique to you and a beautiful part of becoming a woman. Celebrate your individuality and the amazing things your body can do! Remember, there's no one "right" way to look – embrace your unique figure and the strength and beauty it represents.

Skin changes:

Hormonal fluctuations can sometimes lead to oily skin and occasional breakouts. Don't despair, brave adventurer! Developing a healthy skincare routine can help manage these changes. Think of it as giving your skin superpowers – gentle cleansers, moisturizers, and sun protection keeps it healthy and glowing. Remember, everyone experiences skin changes differently, so find what works best for you, and don't be afraid to ask for advice from a trusted adult or dermatologist.

But what about how you are doing emotionally?

Mood swings:

Imagine your emotions are on a rollercoaster, sometimes soaring high and other times dipping low. This is because of those mischievous tricksters called hormones! Mood swings are normal during puberty, but if they feel overwhelming, there are ways to cope. Talking to a friend, journaling, or engaging in calming activities like yoga or meditation can help you navigate these emotional waves.

Remember, you're not alone in this – everyone experiences mood swings during puberty, and together, we can find healthy ways to manage them.

Newfound confidence:

As you explore your talents and interests, discover your strengths, and learn more about yourself, you'll start to develop a powerful sense of self-worth and confidence. Think of it like unlocking a superpower – believing in yourself, standing up for your beliefs, and chasing your dreams! Embrace this newfound confidence and use it to shine brightly in the world. Remember, you are amazing and capable, and you have the power to achieve anything you set your mind to.

Identity exploration:

Who am I? What do I believe in? These are natural questions to ask yourself during puberty. It's an exciting time to experiment with different interests, make new friends, and discover what makes you unique. Don't be afraid to try new things, find your voice, and explore different hobbies and activities. Remember, there's no single answer to the question of who you are – it's a journey of self-discovery, and every experience shapes you into the amazing person you're becoming. Embrace the exploration, celebrate your individuality, and remember, you've got this!

14
HEALTHY HABITS FOR A HAPPY BODY

Well, guess what, adventurer? You have incredible superpowers within you, too, and they're all connected to your amazing body! Just like a superhero needs to train and care for their body to use their powers, you need to develop healthy habits to feel your best and unlock your full potential.

Think of puberty as a super cool training program for your body. It's a time of incredible growth and change, and just as any athlete, you need the right fuel and tools to handle it all. This chapter is your guide to becoming a health ninja, mastering awesome habits like believing in yourself, and becoming ready to conquer anything!

Don't worry; these habits aren't about boring restrictions or impossible challenges. They're about making small, positive changes that will make a big difference in how you feel. Imagine it like adding awesome power-ups to your daily routine, making you feel energized, focused, and ready to tackle any adventure life throws your way!

So, what kind of "power-ups" are we talking about? Here's a sneak peek:

Fuel Your Body:

Think of your body as a super cool machine that needs the right fuel to run at its best. Choose healthy foods like fruits, veggies, whole grains, and lean proteins – they'll give you sustained energy and keep your brain sharp for school, sports, and all your amazing activities. Remember, sugary treats and processed snacks might seem tempting, but they're like temporary bursts of energy that leave you feeling tired later. Choose wisely, adventurer, and fuel your body for greatness!

- **Become a Kitchen Explorer:** Instead of grabbing the usual snacks, raid the fridge and create mini fruit kebabs, colorful veggie sticks with yogurt dip, or even whip up a smoothie packed with healthy ingredients. Experiment, have fun, and discover amazing new flavors that nourish your body!
- **Pack Your Power Lunch:** Ditch the pre-packaged options and pack a lunchbox bursting with superhero fuel. Think whole-wheat sandwiches with lean protein, fresh fruits and veggies, and healthy snacks like nuts or homemade trail mix. Remember, a colorful and nutritious lunch keeps your energy levels soaring throughout the day!

- **Hydration Hero:** Water is your body's best friend! Carry a reusable water bottle and sip throughout the day to stay hydrated and energized. Imagine it like giving your cells a refreshing superpower boost! Avoid sugary drinks that can leave you feeling sluggish and dehydrated.

Move Your Body:

Exercise isn't just about punishment – it's a celebration of your amazing body's abilities! Find activities you enjoy, whether it's dancing, playing sports, swimming, or even taking a brisk walk with a friend. Moving your body helps you stay strong, improves your mood, and even boosts your brainpower. Think of it as activating hidden superpowers – strength, agility, and a happy, healthy mind!

- **Find Your Groove:** Don't consider exercise a chore – make it an adventure! Turn up the music and have a dance party in your room, organize a game of tag with friends, or explore a new hiking trail. Find activities you genuinely enjoy and move your body in ways that make you feel happy and energized.
- **Challenge Accepted!:** Embrace friendly competition! Organize mini sports tournaments with friends, join a school team, or try a new physical activity like rock climbing or swimming. Remember, pushing your limits (safely!) and challenging yourself helps you discover your hidden strengths and builds confidence.
- **Active Breaks Are Awesome!:** Sitting for long periods can drain your energy. Break up your studies or screen time with quick bursts of activity. Do some jumping jacks, take

a walk around the block, or even climb the stairs a few times. These mini-movement breaks will keep your energy levels up and your mind focused.

Sleep Like a Superhero:

Sleep is your body's time to recharge and rebuild. Aim for 9-12 hours of sleep each night to wake up feeling refreshed, energized, and ready to conquer the day. Think of it like a superhero recharging their super suit – sleep gives you the power to focus, learn, and be your best self. So, ditch the late-night screen time and create a relaxing bedtime routine for a super sleep adventure!

- **Create a Calming Retreat**: Make your bedroom a sleep sanctuary. Dim the lights, put away electronics at least an hour before bed, and listen to calming music or read a book. This creates a relaxing atmosphere that signals to your body it's time to wind down.

- **Develop a Bedtime Routine:** Just like superheroes have their pre-mission rituals, create a relaxing bedtime routine. Take a warm bath, write in a journal, or practice calming stretches. Consistency helps your body and mind recognize it's time for sleep.

- **Darkness is Your Ally:** Make sure your bedroom is dark, quiet, and cool for optimal sleep. Darkness triggers the production of melatonin, a hormone that helps you sleep soundly. Ditch the nightlights and create a sleep haven for your superhero rest!

Mindfulness Matters:

Are you feeling stressed or overwhelmed? Take a deep breath, adventurer! Mindfulness practices like meditation, yoga, or simply focusing on your breath can help you calm your mind and manage emotions. Think of it like clearing your mind of negative thoughts and distractions, allowing you to focus on the present moment and find inner peace. Remember, a calm and centered mind is a powerful tool for navigating the ups and downs of life.

- **Breathe Away Stress:** Feeling overwhelmed? Take a few deep breaths, adventurer! Close your eyes, focus on inhaling and exhaling, and let go of any tension. Deep breathing calms your mind and body, helping you manage stress and navigate challenging situations.

- **Gratitude is a Superpower:** Take a moment each day to appreciate the good things in your life. Write down three things you're grateful for, big or small. This simple practice shifts your focus to the positive, boosting your mood and inner peace.

- **Connect with Nature:** Go for a walk in the park, sit under a tree, or listen to the sounds of nature. Immersing yourself in nature has a calming effect, reducing stress and anxiety while promoting mindfulness and well-being.

Remember, adventurer, you have the power to create healthy habits that make you feel amazing! Start small, experiment, have fun, and celebrate your progress. Soon, you'll be a master of your health, radiating confidence and using your superpowers to conquer every challenge with a smile. So, embark on this healthy adventure, one positive step at a time, and remember, you've got this...You have the strength, the potential, and the incredible superpowers within you to create a happy and healthy life!

15

THE MIRROR CHALLENGE: BUILDING SELF-CONFIDENCE

Welcome to a special chapter all about YOU – your unique growth, your inner beauty, and the amazing journey of building self-confidence during puberty. We're diving into "The Mirror Challenge," and trust us, it's a challenge you're going to conquer with flying colors!

The Mirror, Your Friendly Reflection...

As you journey through puberty, you might find yourself spending a little more time in front of the mirror, and that's completely normal. The mirror reflects not just your physical changes but also the incredible person you are becoming on the inside. It's like a magical portal to self-discovery.

Embracing Your Unique Growth:

Puberty brings about changes in your body, and every girl's experience is as unique as a fingerprint. You might notice differences in height, the development of curves, and maybe even the appearance of body hair. This is YOUR unique growth story, and it's a beautiful, one-of-a-kind journey.

Now, let's talk about the Mirror Challenge. Stand in front of the mirror, look yourself in the eyes, and say something positive about yourself. It could be a compliment, a reminder of your strengths, or an acknowledgment of something you love about your personality. Repeat this exercise regularly, and watch your self-confidence grow.

Appreciating Your Inner Beauty:

Mirror, mirror on the wall, who's the most amazing of them all? It's YOU! Your inner beauty shines brighter than any physical changes you're going through. Kindness, compassion, creativity – these qualities make you truly special. Celebrate your unique talents and the wonderful person you are inside.

Healthy Habits for a Healthy You:

Taking care of your body is an essential part of healthy growth. Remember these habits:

- <u>Balanced Nutrition:</u> Eat a variety of foods to give your body the nutrients it needs to grow. Make fruits, vegetables, and whole grains your everyday superheroes!

- Stay Active: Find activities you enjoy, whether it's dancing, playing sports, or going for a walk. Exercise is not just great for your body; it's a mood booster, too!

- Hydration: Drink plenty of water. It's like a secret potion for keeping your skin glowing and your body feeling fantastic.

- Adequate Sleep: Your body does some serious growing while you sleep. Aim for 9-12 hours of sleep each night to wake up refreshed and ready to conquer the day.

Navigating Emotional Changes:

Puberty also brings emotional changes, and it's perfectly okay to feel a whirlwind of emotions. Whether it's excitement, frustration, or everything in between, know that you're not alone. Talk to someone you trust – a friend, family member, or even a teacher – about what you're going through.

The Mirror Challenge is about seeing yourself with kindness and embracing the incredible person you are becoming. Remember, you are on an unstoppable journey, and every step, every change, is a part of your unique story. Be proud, be confident, and most importantly, be true to yourself!

Now, let's talk about the changes you might see in the mirror – the curves, the new heights, and even the tiny freckles. These changes are signs of growth, not just physically but emotionally and mentally, too. Embrace them as milestones on your journey to becoming the incredible person you're destined to be.

Surrounding Yourself with Positivity:

The Mirror Challenge isn't just about what you see; it's also about what you feel. Surround yourself with positivity – whether it's uplifting music, inspiring books, or spending time with people who make you feel good about yourself. Your environment plays a big role in shaping your confidence.

Unleashing Your Superpowers:

Guess what? Puberty comes with some incredible superpowers. Your brain is growing, and so are your abilities. Discover your talents, explore your interests, and let your passions shine. The more you embrace the amazing things you can do, the more confident you'll feel.

Embracing Uniqueness:

Every girl's Mirror Challenge is unique because every girl is unique. Embrace the things that make you different, whether it's your style, your hobbies, or your quirks. Your individuality is your strength, and it's what makes you stand out in the most fantastic way.

Talking About It:

If the Mirror Challenge ever feels like a tough one, remember that you're not alone. Talk to friends, family, or a trusted adult about how you're feeling. Sharing your thoughts and experiences can be a powerful way to gain perspective and support.

Setting Realistic Goals:

Challenge yourself to set small, achievable goals. Whether it's trying something new, accomplishing a task, or even complimenting a friend, these little victories build up and contribute to a growing sense of self-confidence. Celebrate every success along the way!

Cultivating Self-Love:

Above all, the Mirror Challenge is an invitation to cultivate self-love. Treat yourself with kindness and understanding. Focus on the things you love about yourself and the qualities that make you a wonderful person. When you look in the mirror, you see a friend who deserves love and appreciation.

The Unstoppable Girl You Are:

As you stand before the mirror, remember that you are an unstoppable force of nature. The Mirror Challenge isn't just about what you see on the surface; it's about recognizing the strength, resilience, and beauty within. Your journey through puberty is a transformative adventure, and you are the heroine of your own story.

16

FRIENDS FOREVER: NAVIGATING SOCIAL CHANGES

As you journey through puberty, you'll find that your relationships with friends might go through some transformations, and that's absolutely okay. Let's embark on this adventure together and explore the beauty of friendships that can last a lifetime.

Puberty can bring different changes to everyone at different times. Your friends may be experiencing their own unique journeys. Some might be talking about new interests and hobbies, or even sharing thoughts and questions about puberty. Embrace these changes together and remember that open communication is the key to understanding each other.

Communication is Key:

Friendships thrive on communication. Share your thoughts, feelings, and experiences with your friends, and encourage them to do the same. Honest conversations build trust and create a supportive space where you can navigate the ups and downs of growing up together.

Expanding Your Circle:

As you grow, your interests may broaden, and you might discover new passions. Don't be afraid to explore different activities and make new friends. Your social circle can expand, providing you with a diverse tapestry of friendships that enrich your life.

Empathy and Understanding:

Friendship is a two-way street, and empathy plays a crucial role. Understand that everyone experiences puberty differently, and emotions can be a rollercoaster. Be there for your friends, offer support, and practice kindness. In return, you'll find a network of friends who support you during your own journey.

Dealing with Differences:

Just like a tapestry has various patterns and colors, your friend group may have different personalities, interests, and opinions. Embrace these differences, as they add depth and richness to your friendships. Celebrate the uniqueness of each friend and cherish the diversity within your group.

Handling Conflict:

Friendships may encounter challenges, and that's okay. If conflicts arise, approach them with understanding and a willingness to listen. Open and honest communication can resolve misunderstandings and strengthen your bonds. Remember, challenges are opportunities for growth.

Building a Supportive Community:

Your friends are like a built-in support system, ready to celebrate your victories and stand by you during tough times. Cultivate a sense of community where everyone feels valued and supported. Your friendships can be a source of strength and joy throughout your journey.

Friendships forged during puberty can be powerful and enduring. While some aspects of your life may change, the bonds of true friendship can withstand the test of time. Cherish the moments you spend with your friends, create lasting memories, and remember that the best is yet to come.

As you navigate the social changes that come with growing up, know that your friendships are an integral part of your unstoppable journey. Each friend is a unique thread in the tapestry of your life, weaving a story of shared laughter, shared tears, and shared growth.

Friendship isn't just one-on-one; it can also blossom within a group. You might have a close-knit circle of friends or be part of a larger group where everyone brings something special to the table. Embrace the dynamics of group friendship, where different personalities blend together to create a vibrant social mosaic.

Nurturing Individual Friendships:

While group friendships are wonderful, don't forget the beauty of one-on-one connections. Spending quality time with a friend individually allows for deeper conversations and strengthens the unique bond you share. Whether it's a movie night, a walk in the park, or a heart-to-heart chat, cherish these moments.

Peer Pressure and Being True to Yourself:

During puberty, you might encounter new experiences and situations where peer pressure becomes a factor. Stay true to yourself and your values. Real friends respect your choices and don't push you to do uncomfortable things. Surround yourself with friends who appreciate you for being you.

Growing Together, Growing Apart:

As you navigate the twists and turns of friendships, remember that it's okay for people to change and grow. Some friendships may strengthen, and others might naturally drift apart. Both are part of the journey. Celebrate the growth you experience together, and if paths diverge, cherish the memories you've created.

Including Everyone:

In the tapestry of friendship, inclusion is key. Be mindful of others who may feel left out or new friends who join your group. Welcoming everyone with kindness creates an atmosphere where everyone feels valued and accepted. Your actions can make a big difference in someone's day.

Being a Supportive Friend:

Puberty brings challenges and triumphs for everyone. Being a supportive friend means lending a listening ear, offering encouragement, and being there through thick and thin. Your support contributes to the strength of your friendships and creates a positive environment for everyone.

Celebrating Achievements:

Friendship is a journey where you witness each other's growth and accomplishments. Celebrate your friends' achievements, whether big or small. Sharing in each other's joys creates a bond that deepens over time.

The Unstoppable Bond:

Friendship is a bond that withstands the tests of time. As you grow, your friendships evolve into a powerful force. They become a source of comfort, laughter, and shared understanding. Embrace the unstoppable bond that weaves through the tapestry of your life.

Remember, friendships forged during puberty have the potential to last a lifetime. The experiences you share, the challenges you overcome together, and the laughter that echoes through the years create an everlasting thread connecting you to the past, present, and future.

17

CRUSH CHRONICLES: NAVIGATING RELATIONSHIPS

Remember all those amazing discoveries we made about ourselves during puberty? Now, get ready to explore another exciting chapter: relationships! Whether it's butterflies-in-your-tummy crushes, awesome friendships, or even navigating family dynamics, relationships are a big part of our lives. But don't worry; we're here to guide you through it all like the rockstar you are!

Think of this chapter as your backstage pass to the world of relationships. We'll explore different types of friendships, learn how to handle tricky situations, and discover the joys and challenges of crushes. Remember, every relationship is unique, and there's no one "right" way to navigate them. The most important thing is to be yourself, communicate openly, and treat others with respect.

So, grab your backstage pass, and let's dive in…

First Stop: Friendship Frenzy!

Friends are like awesome bandmates supporting you on your adventure! They make you laugh, cheer you up, and celebrate your victories. Here are some tips for rocking your friendships:

- **Be a Good Listener**: Lend an ear when your friends need you, just like you'd want them to do for you.
- **Be Trustworthy**: Keep secrets and promises and be someone your friends can rely on.
- Celebrate Differences: Embrace what makes each friend unique.
- **Communicate Openly:** Talk about your feelings honestly and respectfully, even when it's difficult.
- **Respect Boundaries:** Everyone needs some space sometimes. Be understanding and supportive.

Next Level: Dealing with Disagreements:

Even rockstars have occasional off-key moments. Don't worry; disagreements are normal in any relationship. Here's how to handle them like a pro:

- **Stay Calm:** Take a deep breath and avoid getting angry or impulsive.

- **Listen to Understand:** Try to see things from your friend's perspective.
- **Communicate Clearly:** Express your feelings and needs in a respectful way.
- **Find Common Ground:** Look for solutions that work for everyone.

Remember, Friendship Matters: Don't let disagreements break your bond.

The Spotlight on Crushes:

Butterflies-in-your-tummy, daydreaming, and maybe even a little nervousness – that's the amazing (and sometimes confusing) world of crushes! Here's how to navigate them with confidence:

- **Be Yourself:** Don't try to be someone you're not to impress someone. The right person will love you for who you are.
- **Take Things Slow:** Get to know the person before jumping into deep feelings.
- **Respect Their Feelings:** Don't pressure them or expect anything in return for your emotions.
- **Enjoy the Journey:** Crushes can be fun and exciting, even if they don't always lead to a relationship.

Remember, You're Amazing: Whether someone likes you back or not, your worth never changes!

Those butterflies-in-your-tummy crushes? They can be exciting, confusing, and even overwhelming! It's totally normal to experience a rollercoaster of emotions, from blissful joy to sadness. But don't worry; we're here to help you navigate it all like a pro!

First, let's identify those confusing feelings. Feeling butterflies when you see your crush? That's your happy hormones doing their thing! Embrace it, but remember, excitement can sometimes make you act impulsively. Take a breath and stay grounded. Are you feeling nervous or shy? It's normal! Everyone gets nervous sometimes. Use humor or take deep breaths to manage your nerves.

Does your crush like you back?

Trying to decipher mixed messages can be tough. Don't overthink it! Talk to a trusted friend or simply focus on being yourself. Seeing your crush interact with someone else can sting, but remember, everyone has the right to socialize. Instead of jealousy, focus on building your own positive relationships. Facing rejection can feel painful, but it's an inevitable part of life. Remember, it doesn't define your worth! Lean on your friends, remind yourself of your awesomeness, and don't be afraid to try again.

Crushes can bring out a whirlwind of emotions, so self-care is crucial! Share your feelings with a trusted friend, family member, or therapist. Sometimes, just talking things through can help you gain clarity and perspective. Express yourself through writing, drawing, singing, or dancing – unleash your emotions in a healthy way. Don't neglect your hobbies and interests! Focusing on the things that bring you joy helps maintain your emotional balance. Be kind to yourself, adventurer! Treat yourself with the same compassion you would offer a friend.

Crushes are exciting, but don't let them define you. You are an amazing, unique individual with so much to offer the world! Remember, your worth is constant, whether someone likes you back or not. You are worthy of love and respect, always. Focus on what makes you shine! Spend time developing your talents, exploring your passions, and building strong friendships. This inner confidence will attract people who appreciate you for who you truly are.

Enjoy the journey!

Don't put pressure on yourself to rush into anything. Embrace the experience of having a crush, learn from it, and grow as a person.

18

CYBER SPACE: NAVIGATING SOCIAL MEDIA

As you grow up, you'll find that connecting with friends online becomes a part of your life. Let's embark on this digital adventure together and discover how to navigate the vast landscape of social media with wisdom, kindness, and confidence.

The Digital Playground:

Think of social media as a digital playground where you can share moments and ideas and connect with friends, near and far. It's a space where creativity, self-expression, and friendship flourish. But, like any playground, it comes with its own set of rules and responsibilities.

There are various social media platforms, each with its own features and vibes. From Instagram's visual storytelling to TikTok's short videos and Facebook's broad connections, understanding how these platforms work helps you make the most of your online experience.

Be Your Authentic Self:

In the vast world of Cyber Space, authenticity shines the brightest. Be true to yourself online, just as you are offline. Share your interests, thoughts, and experiences genuinely. Your uniqueness is your superpower, and it deserves to be celebrated.

Mindful Posting:

Before hitting that post button, take a moment to think about what you're sharing. Ensure your content reflects the positive and amazing person you are. Remember, once something is online, it can be challenging to take back. Be kind, respectful, and mindful of your digital footprint.

Privacy Matters:

Your privacy is essential. Understand the privacy settings on your social media accounts and choose what you share wisely. Be cautious about sharing personal information and ensure that your online space feels safe and secure.

Cyberbullying Awareness:

Cyberbullying is never okay. If you witness or experience any form of online negativity, speak up and report it. Create a culture of kindness and support within your digital community. Your online space should be a reflection of the positive and uplifting person you are.

While social media is a fantastic way to connect, balancing your screen time is crucial. Spend quality moments in the real world – enjoy outdoor activities, face-to-face conversations, and hobbies that bring you joy. Finding this balance ensures a healthy relationship with technology.

Online Friendships:

Making friends online is common, but it's essential to be cautious. Talk to your parents or a trusted adult about your online connections. Remember that true friendships, whether online or offline, should be built on trust, respect, and genuine connection.

Digital Well-being:

Your well-being matters in both the physical and digital realms. If you ever feel overwhelmed or stressed by social media, take a step back. Prioritize self-care, talk to someone you trust, and remember that your value goes far beyond likes, comments, or follower counts.

Navigating Challenges:

Just like in the real world, challenges may arise in Cyberspace. Whether it's dealing with online drama, handling misunderstandings, or simply feeling overwhelmed, know that you're not alone. Reach out to friends, family, or a trusted adult for guidance.

As you navigate the vast and ever-evolving world of Cyber Space, remember that you are in control. You have the power to create a positive, supportive, and authentic digital experience. Be the unstoppable force for good in cyberspace, and let your online journey be a reflection of the incredible girl you are becoming.

Practicing good digital etiquette in this expansive digital playground is as crucial as being kind in the real world. Respond to comments and messages with politeness, avoid oversharing personal details, and remember that your online interactions shape your digital reputation.

The Power of Positivity:

In the digital realm, positivity is a superpower. Share uplifting content, compliment others, and create an online atmosphere that radiates kindness. Your positive presence can inspire others and contribute to a harmonious Cyberspace.

Embracing Differences:

Social media connects people from diverse backgrounds and cultures. Embrace these differences, learn from others, and celebrate the beauty of a global community. Remember, your digital interactions have the potential to break down barriers and foster understanding.

Setting Boundaries:

Just like in the physical world, it's crucial to establish healthy boundaries online. Decide how much time you want to spend on social media, when to take breaks, and when it's best to disconnect. Setting boundaries ensures that your digital adventure remains a positive and enriching experience.

Unplugging for Self-Care:

Amidst the excitement of cyberspace, don't forget the importance of unplugging for self-care. Take breaks from screens, engage in activities you love, and nurture your mental and emotional well-being. The real world holds countless wonders waiting to be explored.

Building a Positive Community:

Be a digital trailblazer by actively contributing to building a positive online community. Encourage friends to share their talents, support each other's endeavors, and create a space where everyone feels valued. Together, you can shape a CyberSpace that reflects the unstoppable force of positivity.

Creative Expression:

Social media is an excellent platform for expressing your creativity. Whether it's through art, writing, or sharing your interests, let your imagination soar. Use your unique voice to make a positive impact, inspiring others to embrace their creativity as well.

Digital Leadership:

As you grow in Cyber Space, you become a digital leader. Lead by example, promote positivity, and encourage others to use social media as a tool for good. Your actions can inspire a generation of digital users to make the internet a better place for everyone.

Lifelong Learning:

The world of technology is ever-evolving, and there's always something new to discover. Stay curious, be open to learning, and explore the digital landscape with a sense of wonder. Lifelong learning in Cyber Space ensures that you remain savvy and adaptable in the online world.

Reflection and Growth:

Your journey in Cyberspace is a continuous process of reflection and growth. Learn from your experiences, celebrate your achievements, and navigate challenges with resilience. Just as in the real world, each moment in Cyber Space contributes to the incredible person you are becoming.

So, dear girls, remember the power you hold to shape your digital narrative as you continue your unstoppable adventure in cyberspace. Be authentic, be kind, and let your online presence sparkle with the uniqueness that defines you. Your journey in Cyber Space is not just about navigating the digital landscape – it's about leaving a positive and lasting impact on the world.

19

#BODYPOSITIVITY: LOVING YOUR UNIQUE SELF

All Bodies are Beautiful

Ditch the Drama, Embrace the Magic: Unleashing Your Inner Body Rockstar!

Forget flipping through magazines filled with airbrushed perfection, adventurer! Ditch the unrealistic expectations and the constant internal critic. It's time to rewrite the script and become the star of your own body positivity show!

Remember how we conquered puberty like total rockstars? Now, get ready to rock a different stage – the stage of loving and appreciating your incredible, unique self, flaws, and all! No more hiding, shrinking, or comparing yourself to some impossible ideal. It's time to unleash your inner body rockstar and strut your stuff with confidence that shines brighter than any spotlight.

This chapter isn't about boring lectures or restrictive diets. It's about unlocking the superpower of self-love and discovering the magic that radiates from embracing your unique beauty. We'll explore why body positivity is your backstage pass to happiness, learn how to silence the negative noise, and celebrate the incredible features that make you YOU!

So, grab your metaphorical mic, adventurer, and get ready to sing your body's praises! We're here to cheer you on as you rewrite the beauty narrative, own your individuality, and rock your body with fierce confidence. Remember, you are strong, beautiful, and worthy of love, just the way you are. Let's rewrite the script and turn the world into your personal stage!

Now, let's dive into another crucial mission: body positivity! Forget unrealistic beauty standards and societal pressures – it's time to celebrate our amazing bodies and rock them confidently!

Think of this chapter as your backstage pass to self-love and acceptance. We'll explore why body positivity matters, discover ways to appreciate your unique features, and learn how to shut down negative self-talk. Remember, your body is your incredible instrument, carrying you through life's adventures. Treat it with kindness and respect and watch your confidence soar!

Why Body Positivity Rocks:

First, why is body positivity so important? Here are just a few reasons:

- **It boosts your confidence:** When you appreciate your body, you radiate confidence that shines through in everything you do.

- **It improves your mental health:** Accepting your body reduces stress, anxiety, and unhealthy comparisons to others.

- **It empowers you to make healthy choices:** You're more likely to nourish your body with good food and move it in ways you enjoy when you appreciate it.

- **It challenges unrealistic beauty standards:** We come in all shapes, sizes, and colors, and that's beautiful! Let's break free from unrealistic expectations and celebrate our unique diversity.

Discovering Your Inner Rockstar:

Now, how do we cultivate this awesome body positivity? Here's your backstage guide:

- **Focus on your strengths:** What do you love about your body? It could be your strong legs, dazzling smile, or infectious laugh. Celebrate those features!

- **Challenge negative thoughts:** When negative self-talk creeps in, replace it with positive affirmations. Remind yourself of your awesomeness!

- **Surround yourself with positivity:** Ditch the negativity and surround yourself with people who appreciate you for who you are, inside and out.

- **Embrace your individuality:** We are all unique and beautiful in our own way. Celebrate what makes you stand out, whether your freckles, curly hair, or quirky dance moves!

- **Nourish your body:** Treat your body like the incredible machine it is by fueling it with healthy foods and moving it in ways you enjoy. Exercise isn't about punishment; it's about celebrating your body's capabilities!

Remember, You're the Star of the Show:

Body positivity is a journey, not a destination. There will be ups and downs, but don't give up! Here are some final words of encouragement:

- **It's okay to have flaws:** We all do! What matters is how we treat ourselves and others.

- **Progress, not perfection:** Focus on celebrating small victories, like trying a new healthy recipe or wearing an outfit you love.

- **Love yourself unconditionally:** You are worthy of love and respect, no matter what. Treat yourself with the same kindness you would offer your best friend.

This body positivity journey isn't a sprint; it's an epic adventure! There will be bumps along the way, moments of self-doubt, and days when the negative voices try to creep in. But here's the secret weapon you always have: YOU!

You are strong and capable and have the power to silence the negativity and rewrite your own story. When self-doubt whispers, drown it out with a roar of self-love. When comparisons cloud your vision, remember your unique beauty shines brighter than any manufactured ideal.

Embrace the journey, celebrate the victories (big and small!), and know that you're never alone. Surround yourself with people who see your worth and encourage your self-love. Share your struggles, celebrate your wins, and be a shining example of body positivity for others.

Remember, you are an incredible creation, a masterpiece in your own right. So, adventurer, own your spotlight, rock your unique body with confidence, and spread the message of self-love wherever you go. The world needs your sparkle, your authenticity, and your unwavering belief in yourself. Shine on, adventurer, and remember, you've got this!

And one last thing: As you step off the stage and continue your adventure, remember your worth is never defined by a number on a scale, a size in a clothing tag, or someone else's opinion. You are worthy, you are strong, and you are beautiful, just the way you are.

20

FOOD FUEL: EATING RIGHT FOR PUBERTY

In the magical journey through puberty, your body is like a superhero gearing up for incredible adventures. And what does every superhero need? The right kind of nutrition! Check out this table for fun and tasty options that will fuel your body with the nutrients it needs during this exciting time.

Imagine your plate as a superhero's power-up station, filled with vibrant colors, tasty textures, and the essential nutrients your body needs to thrive. We've curated a table of delightful options that not only make your taste buds dance but also ensure your body gets the superhero fuel it deserves.

From Rainbow Smoothies that bring a burst of vitamins to Chickpea Wraps packed with protein power, each food group plays a unique role in supporting your growth and well-being. Get ready to explore the world of nutrient-rich delights, turning your meals into a celebration of health and flavor.

This table serves as your handy guide to the essential nutrients needed during this exciting phase, along with delicious food examples to power your adventures:

Nutrient	Importance for Puberty	Delicious Food Sources
Calcium	Strong bones and teeth, healthy nerve, and muscle function	Dairy products (milk, cheese, yogurt), fortified plant-based milks, leafy greens (kale, spinach), tofu
Vitamin D	Helps your body absorb calcium, supports bone health	Fatty fish (salmon, tuna), egg yolks, fortified foods (milk, cereals), sunshine!
Iron	Carries oxygen in the blood and supports energy levels	Lean meats (beef, chicken), fish, beans, lentils, dark leafy greens, fortified cereals
Protein	Builds and repairs tissues, supports growth and development	Lean meats (chicken, fish), eggs, beans, lentils, nuts, seeds, tofu
Healthy Fats	Supports brain development, promotes satiety, and cell growth	Nuts, seeds, avocado, olive oil, fatty fish

Fiber	Aids digestion, keeps you feeling full, promotes gut health	Fruits, vegetables, whole grains (brown rice, quinoa, whole-wheat bread)
Vitamins & Minerals	Support overall health and development	Varies by vitamin/mineral (see chart below)

But what about the other kinds of powerhouses?

Vitamin/ Mineral	Importance	Food Sources
Vitamin A	Healthy vision, immune function	Sweet potatoes, carrots, spinach, cantaloupe
Vitamin C	Immune function, collagen production	Citrus fruits, bell peppers, broccoli
Vitamin B12	Energy production, nervous system function	Meat, fish, eggs, fortified plant-based milk
Zinc	Growth and development, immune function	Meat, poultry, seafood, beans, nuts
Folate	Cell growth, red blood cell production	Leafy greens, beans, lentils, fortified cereals

And don't be scared if it seems too much to take care of all by yourself. You just have to keep reading for all the simple ideas and go-to snacks that our healthy recipe for a healthy body can create.

Remember, adventurers, puberty is a time of incredible growth and change, and your body needs the right fuel to power through it all! Forget boring salads and bland meals – let's explore some fun and delicious options that are packed with the nutrients you need to thrive.

Breakfast Power-Ups:

1. Smoothie Bowl Extravaganza: Blend your favorite fruits (berries, mango, banana) with yogurt or milk, and top with granola, nuts, seeds, and a drizzle of honey.

2. Scrambled Egg Fiesta: Whip up scrambled eggs with chopped veggies (spinach, mushrooms, bell peppers) and cheese for a protein-packed start. Add a whole-wheat toast or wrap on the side.

3. Overnight Oats Adventure: Mix rolled oats, yogurt, milk, chia seeds, and your favorite flavorings (fruits, nuts, spices) the night before for a grab-and-go breakfast with fiber and healthy fats.

Lunchbox Legends:

1. Rainbow Veggie Wraps: Fill whole-wheat tortillas with colorful veggies (cucumber, carrots, lettuce, hummus), lean protein (grilled chicken, tuna salad), and a sprinkle of cheese.

2. DIY Lunchable Fun: Skip the processed versions and create your own! Pack mini cherry tomatoes, baby carrots, whole-wheat crackers, slices of cheese, and a hard-boiled egg for a satisfying and fun lunch.

3. Pasta Primavera Surprise: Make whole-wheat pasta with a light tomato sauce, add in a variety of cooked veggies (broccoli, peas, corn), and sprinkle with Parmesan cheese for a quick and filling meal.

Snacktastic Treats:

1. DIY Trail Mix: Grab a container and mix nuts, seeds, dried fruit, and even some dark chocolate chips for a sweet and crunchy snack packed with healthy fats and energy.

2. Frozen Yogurt Parfaits: Layer plain yogurt with granola, fresh fruit slices, and a drizzle of honey for a cool and refreshing treat.

3. Apple & Peanut Butter Smiles: Slice apples and pair them with peanut butter for a classic, protein-rich snack. Get creative with different nut butters or add a sprinkle of cinnamon for extra flavor.

Don't Forget These Superheroes:

1. Fruits: Nature's candy! Munch on colorful fruits throughout the day for vitamins, minerals, and fiber.

2. Vegetables: Power up your plate with vibrant veggies at every meal. Try roasting them, grilling them, or blending them into smoothies for variety.

3. Whole Grains: Opt for whole-wheat bread, brown rice, quinoa, and oats for sustained energy and essential nutrients.

4. Lean Protein: Chicken, fish, beans, lentils, and tofu provide building blocks for growth and keep you feeling full.

5. Healthy Fats: Include nuts, seeds, avocado, and olive oil in your diet for brain health, energy, and satiety.

Remember, adventurers, eating right isn't about restriction; it's about fueling your body for amazing adventures! Experiment, have fun, and choose foods that make you feel energized, happy, and ready to conquer anything!

21

SLEEP SECRETS: BEAUTY REST FOR GROWING BODIES

Imagine sleep as a spell that transforms tiredness into renewed energy, stress into calm, and chaos into order. Your growing body is like a superhero in need of recharging, and sleep is the invisible force that empowers you for the challenges and triumphs that await each day.

The Puberty Pillow Talk

During puberty, your body undergoes remarkable changes, and sleep is the magical potion that supports this transformation. It's not just about resting your eyes; it's about giving your body the time it needs to grow, heal, and flourish. Let's dive into the secrets that make sleep an essential element in your journey.

Sleep is the prime time for your body to experience growth spurts. Human Growth Hormone (HGH), the superhero of growth, is released during deep sleep, ensuring that your body develops at its own unstoppable pace.

Have you ever wondered how wizards enhance their magical abilities? Well, sleep is your brain's potion for boosting memory, learning, and problem-solving skills. A well-rested mind is a sharp mind, ready to conquer the challenges of each day.

Hormone Harmony:

Puberty brings a dance of hormones, and sleep is the choreographer that ensures harmony. Adequate sleep regulates hormones like cortisol and insulin, contributing to a balanced mood, healthy weight, and overall well-being.

Skin Magic:

Are you dreaming of radiant skin? Sleep is your beauty rest, promoting the production of collagen and elastin – the magical ingredients for healthy and glowing skin. Say hello to your natural skincare routine!

Emotional Resilience:

Puberty emotions can be like unpredictable spells. A good night's sleep acts as your shield, enhancing emotional resilience and helping you navigate the ups and downs of adolescence with grace and strength.

The Sleepy Spells Guide

Spell 1: The Sleep Sanctuary:

Create a cozy and calming sleep environment. Dim the lights, add soft bedding, and make your sleep space a sanctuary where dreams weave their magic.

Spell 2: Consistent Rituals:

Craft bedtime rituals that signal your body it's time to wind down. Whether it's reading a magical book, practicing relaxation exercises, or simply taking deep breaths, consistency is the key.

Spell 3: Magical Mattress and Pillows:

Invest in a comfortable mattress and pillows – your trusty companions for a night filled with sweet dreams. Support your growing body with the right sleep gear.

Spell 4: Screen Time Spell-Breaker:

Before bed, break the spell of screen time. The glow of devices can interfere with your body's natural sleep rhythm. Opt for calming activities instead.

Spell 5: Mindful Eating Magic:

Avoid heavy meals close to bedtime. Choose sleep-friendly snacks that won't cast a spell of indigestion on your peaceful night's rest.

In the nocturnal realm, unseen guardians are ensuring your sleep spell remains unbroken. Meet these mystical protectors who work tirelessly to make your nights restful and restorative.

The Sandman:

Legend has it that the Sandman sprinkles magical sand, bringing dreams to slumbering minds. Embrace the gentle embrace of his sand and let the dreams unfold in the canvas of your mind.

Dream Catchers:

Hang a dream catcher by your bedside to capture any wandering worries or restless thoughts. Let its delicate threads filter through the dreams, allowing only the sweet and positive ones to pass.

Moonlight Whispers:

As the moonlight spills through your window, it whispers enchantments to ease your mind. Embrace the calming energy of moonlight, letting it cradle you into a serene and tranquil sleep.

The Sleep Rituals Handbook

Ritual 1: Twilight Reflections:

Before the bedtime hour approaches, take a moment to reflect on the day's adventures. Jot down your thoughts or express them through art. This twilight ritual helps declutter the mind, ensuring a peaceful transition to dreamland.

Ritual 2: Luminescent Library:

Swap the bright screens for the soft glow of a luminescent library. Dive into the pages of a captivating book – your passport to dream worlds and fantastical adventures. Let your imagination soar before the Sandman arrives.

Ritual 3: Celestial Serenade:

As you settle into your cozy sleep sanctuary, invite the celestial serenade into your space. Play soft and calming tunes or nature sounds that mimic the gentle lullabies of the night. Let the melody guide you into a realm of tranquility.

Ritual 4: Starlit Stretches:

Engage in gentle stretches to release the tension accumulated during the day. The starlit stretches pave the way for a relaxed body, ensuring you drift into a deep and rejuvenating slumber.

Ritual 5: Breath of the Night:

Harness the power of the breath of the night. Practice mindful breathing exercises, inhaling the crisp night air and exhaling any lingering stress. This ritual invites serenity, making your journey into the dream world smoother.

The Sleep Chronicles: Record Your Dreams

Embrace the magical art of dream-keeping by creating your own Sleep Chronicles. Before you step into the world of dreams, jot down your thoughts, adventures, and the landscapes you visit during the night. Let your Sleep Chronicles become a treasure trove of nocturnal wonders.

As you awaken from your beauty rest, bask in the magic of a new day. Feel the rejuvenation coursing through your body and carry the enchantment of a well-rested night into the adventures that await.

22

STRESS BUSTERS: COPING WITH THE TEEN TORNADO

Remember how we have slayed the dragons of puberty so far? Now, get ready to tackle another common foe: stress! Yep, school deadlines, family drama, social pressures – it's enough to make anyone feel like a swirling tornado inside. But don't worry; we've got your back!

Think of this chapter as your stress-busting toolkit. We'll explore different types of stress, discover healthy coping mechanisms, and learn how to keep your cool even when things get chaotic. Remember, stress is a normal part of life, but how you handle it matters. So, grab your toolkit, and let's tame that inner tornado together!

- **Say No:** It's okay to say no sometimes! Don't overload yourself with commitments that add to your stress. Learn to prioritize and delegate when needed.

- **Seek Support**: If you're feeling overwhelmed, don't hesitate to seek professional help. Talking to a therapist or counselor can equip you with additional coping mechanisms and support.

Remember, Adventurer, You're in Control…

Stress may knock on your door, but it doesn't have to stay. You can manage stress effectively and maintain your inner peace with the right tools and awareness. Remember:

- Stress is temporary: It may feel intense, but it will pass. Focus on managing it in the moment, and remember, brighter days are ahead.

- You are strong: You've got the power to overcome challenges and navigate difficult situations. Believe in yourself and your ability to cope.

- Seek help when needed: Don't be afraid to ask for support. There are people who care about you and want to help you manage stress in a healthy way.

Imagine, girl warriors, that stress is like a mischievous imp trying to trip you up during your epic adventures. It might throw tests and deadlines your way, whisper insecurities in your ear, or stir up drama with friends. But remember, you're not just any warrior; you're a stress-busting ninja!

Your secret weapon? Your personalized calmness toolkit. Fill it with things that make your heart sing, and your worries shrink. Maybe it's a playlist of empowering anthems, a notebook for journaling your feelings, or a fluffy pet to cuddle when things feel overwhelming. Remember, your toolkit is unique to you, so explore and discover what works best.

When the imp tries its tricks, don't let it catch you off guard. Be a mindfulness master! Take deep breaths, counting each inhale and exhale like a warrior counting her victories. Close your eyes and imagine a peaceful place, a mental haven where the imp's negativity can't reach you. Talk it out with your trusted squad – your friends, family, or a therapist – sharing your worries like battle strategies.

Remember, girl warriors, you're not alone in this fight. There will be days when the imp seems invincible, but don't give up! Seek support, lean on your tribe, and remember your inner strength. You are braver than you believe, stronger than you seem, and wiser than you think.

So, chin up, girl warriors! Equip yourselves with your calmness toolkits, practice your mindfulness techniques, and remember, the imp doesn't stand a chance against your fierce determination and positive spirit.

23

PARENT-TEEN TALKS: BUILDING BRIDGES

Puberty brings about a cascade of changes, not just in your body but also in your emotions, thoughts, and relationships. This chapter is your compass for navigating the conversational pathways with your parents, building bridges of understanding, trust, and open communication.

Your parents have traveled the road of adolescence themselves. Recognizing that they've experienced similar challenges can be the first step in understanding their perspective. Their wisdom can be a beacon guiding you through uncharted waters.

Puberty often unleashes a whirlwind of emotions. Share your feelings with your parents – the excitement, uncertainties, and even the occasional frustrations. Open communication is the bridge that connects your world with theirs.

Listening with Empathy:

Conversations are a two-way street. Practice active listening when your parents share their insights or concerns. Empathizing with their experiences strengthens the connection, fostering an environment where everyone feels heard.

The Empathy Arch:

Step into each other's shoes by creating an empathy arch. Imagine walking through life with their experiences and perspectives. This visualization fosters understanding, breaking down communication barriers.

The Sharing Circle:

Initiate a sharing circle where each family member has the floor to express their thoughts and feelings. This circle promotes a sense of equality, encouraging everyone to contribute to the ongoing conversation.

The Communication Toolkit:

Equip yourself with a communication toolkit. This includes using "I" statements to express your feelings, asking open-ended questions to encourage dialogue, and practicing patience to allow for thoughtful responses.

Navigating Puberty Together:

Recognize that puberty is new territory for both you and your parents. Acknowledge the learning curve and embark on this journey as a team, supporting one another through the twists and turns.

Setting Boundaries and Expectations:

Establish clear boundaries and expectations. Discuss topics such as curfews, responsibilities, and personal space. Mutual agreement on these aspects creates a foundation of trust and understanding.

Celebrating Achievements:

Share your achievements and milestones. Whether big or small, these moments are building blocks in your journey. Celebrating together strengthens the parent-teen bond and creates lasting memories.

The Magic of Understanding

In the realm of puberty, communication is the magic wand that transforms challenges into opportunities for growth. Remember, building bridges is a continuous process. Embrace the ongoing conversation with your parents, weaving a tapestry of shared experiences, laughter, and understanding.

Navigating conversations with parents can sometimes feel like trying to cross a wobbly rope bridge, right? Don't worry; we've got you covered! This table is your handy guide to building strong bridges of communication with your amazing parents, making those sometimes-tricky talks smoother and more productive.

Communication Challenge	Bridge-Building Hack	Why it Works:
Feeling unheard or misunderstood:	Start with "I" statements: Instead of accusatory "you" statements, say "I feel..." and explain your perspective calmly. It shows you're taking responsibility for your feelings.	This helps avoid defensiveness and opens the door for understanding.
Wanting more independence:	Show them you're responsible: Offer to take on more chores, manage your time well, or discuss compromises that demonstrate your maturity.	Shows initiative and trustworthiness, earning their respect and potentially more freedom.
Disagreements about rules or expectations:	Seek common ground: Listen to their concerns and calmly present your side. Suggest solutions that meet both your needs.	Demonstrates you value their perspective and are willing to find win-win solutions.
Feeling pressure to do something you're uncomfortable with:	Be assertive: Clearly and confidently state your boundaries and explain your reasons. Offer alternatives if possible.	Shows respect for yourself and your needs, encouraging open communication.
Wanting more privacy:	Offer compromises: Agree on designated "privacy zones" or times and demonstrate responsible behavior in other areas.	Shows you respect their wishes and are willing to meet them halfway.

Remember, adventurers:

- Communication is a two-way street: Actively listen to your parents and try to understand their point of view.
- Respect matters: Treat each other with courtesy and kindness, even if you disagree.
- Start small: Practice these hacks in everyday conversations to build trust and improve communication gradually.
- Patience is key: Building strong communication takes time and effort, so be patient and persistent.

As you sail through these uncharted waters, the depth of connection you share with your parents becomes the compass guiding you. Dive into conversations not just about the physical changes but also the emotional landscapes. Your parents, once your guides, are now your co-navigators in this sea of transformation.

Puberty brings emotional storms, unpredictable and intense. Share the nuances of these storms with your parents. Let them be the lighthouse, offering guidance and reassurance when the seas get rough. Vulnerability is not a weakness but a bridge to understanding.

The empathy arch you create is a living bridge, evolving with every shared experience. Step onto it not just to understand your parents but also to be understood. Empathy is the mortar that holds the bricks of connection together. It's a bridge that can withstand the tests of time and change.

The sharing circle isn't a one-time event; it's an ongoing flow of thoughts, feelings, and experiences. Make it a regular ritual where everyone has a voice. Like a river, this circle gathers your family's collective wisdom, creating a reservoir of shared understanding.

Your communication toolkit is not static; it evolves with your experiences. Add new tools like compromise, negotiation, and active acknowledgment. As you refine these tools, you become a skilled communicator, capable of navigating the intricate channels of parent-teen conversations.

Navigating puberty together is a team effort. Recognize the collective strength within your family unit. Every challenge faced and conquered becomes a testament to your shared resilience. As a team, you're not just surviving puberty; you're thriving through it.

Clear boundaries are like beacons in the night, guiding the ship safely to the harbor. Establish them with your parents, respecting each other's space and autonomy. These boundaries are not barriers but guidelines ensuring a healthy and respectful coexistence.

Marking Milestones:

The journey through puberty is marked by countless milestones. Celebrate them with your parents – the first steps into newfound responsibilities, the triumphs over challenges, and the joys of personal growth. These shared celebrations forge memories that withstand the tests of time.

In the magical realm of puberty, communication is the alchemy that turns misunderstandings into understanding. Let the conversations with your parents be a blend of honesty, patience, and a sprinkle of humor. The alchemy of understanding transforms the mundane into the extraordinary.

Building bridges isn't a one-time task; it's a continuous weaving of a tapestry. Each thread represents a shared experience, a lesson learned, or a laughter shared. Your tapestry is unique, a masterpiece in the making, reflecting the beauty of family connection.

24

CELEBRATING YOU: EMBRACING INDIVIDUALITY

Hey there, radiant adventurers! Remember how we've conquered dragons, slayed trolls, and navigated the wild landscapes of puberty? Now, it's time for a different kind of adventure: celebrating YOU!

Forget the pressure to fit into some mold or follow the crowd. Forget comparing yourself to others and wishing you were someone you're not. You, my friend, are a unique masterpiece, a beautiful blend of quirks, talents, and dreams that make you shine brighter than any star. It's time to embrace the magic of your individuality and celebrate the person you are, flaws and all!

Think of your individuality as a hidden treasure chest overflowing with sparkling gems. Each gem represents a part of you – your kindness, your humor, your creativity, your passion for music, your love for animals, your goofy laugh. Every gem is precious, contributing to the unique kaleidoscope that is you.

But sometimes, dust and cobwebs can cloud these gems, making them harder to see. Maybe you compare yourself to others, focusing on their seemingly perfect lives instead of your own unique brilliance. Maybe you listen to negative voices that whisper doubts and insecurities. But remember, those voices don't define you. They're just echoes of fear trying to dim your light.

So, let's polish those gems! Here's how:

Shine your light:

What makes you unique? What are you passionate about? What makes you laugh until your belly hurts? Explore your interests, discover your talents, and let your inner spark ignite!

Embrace your quirks:

Don't try to be someone you're not. Celebrate your weirdness, your silliness, your one-of-a-kind laugh. It's those quirks that make you, you!

Be kind to yourself:

Talk to yourself the way you would talk to your best friend. Forgive yourself for mistakes, celebrate your victories, and remember you are worthy of love and respect, just as you are.

Surround yourself with positivity:

Find friends who celebrate your individuality, who lift you up, and who make you feel good about yourself. Ditch the negativity and embrace the sunshine!

Be your own cheerleader:

Don't wait for others to validate you. Believe in yourself, celebrate your achievements, and know that you are capable of amazing things!

Picture this girl warrior: imagine yourself walking through a bustling marketplace, surrounded by stalls overflowing with dazzling trinkets. Each stall represents a different aspect of individuality – a splash of vibrant creativity here, a dash of quirky humor there, a sprinkle of infectious enthusiasm further down. And amidst this vibrant landscape stands YOU, a blank canvas ready to be adorned with the treasures that speak to your soul.

Don't be tempted by the pressure to grab a pre-made "perfect" persona from someone else's stall. Remember, true beauty lies in authenticity, in embracing the unique blend of traits that make you YOU. So, wander through the marketplace with your eyes wide open, drawn to the things that resonate with your deepest desires.

Maybe you pick up a paintbrush and unleash your artistic flair, adding splashes of color to your world. Perhaps you grab a pair of silly socks and rock them with confidence, a reminder that laughter is your superpower. Maybe you choose a book on a fascinating topic, igniting your curiosity and fueling your thirst for knowledge. Every choice you make, every quirk you embrace, adds a precious gem to your own unique masterpiece.

Remember, girl warrior, your flaws are just as important as your strengths. They tell the story of your journey, your battles fought, and lessons learned. Don't let them dim your sparkle. Instead, see them as brushstrokes, adding depth and character to your canvas. Forgive yourself for mistakes, learn from them, and emerge stronger and more radiant than ever before.

Surround yourself with people who appreciate your unique shine. Seek out friends who celebrate your quirks, encourage your dreams, and make you feel like the incredible warrior you are. Ditch the negativity and bask in the warm glow of genuine support. Remember, your tribe is your chosen family, the ones who help you polish your gems and amplify your inner light.

Most importantly, girl warrior, be your own biggest cheerleader. Don't wait for external validation. Look in the mirror and see the strength, the beauty, the potential that shines within you. Believe in your dreams, celebrate your victories (big and small!), and know that you have the power to create a life as magical and dazzling as you are.

So, step into the world with your head held high, your individuality like a banner proudly displayed. Let your laughter ring out, your creativity flow and your unique spirit inspire others. The world needs your sparkle, your authenticity, and the unwavering belief in yourself. Remember, girl warrior, you are a masterpiece in the making.

25

BEYOND PUBERTY: A SNEAK PEEK INTO THE FUTURE

Now, get ready for the most exciting part of the adventure: the future! Yes, adventurer, beyond the rollercoaster ride of puberty, lies a vast landscape filled with possibilities, dreams, and incredible experiences waiting to be explored.

Think of this chapter as your personal roadmap, offering a glimpse into the amazing things that await you. It's not about predicting the exact twists and turns but about igniting your curiosity and empowering you to take charge of your journey.

Picture yourself standing on a mountain peak, gazing out at a vast, uncharted landscape. This is your future, stretching out before you in a dazzling array of possibilities. No longer confined by the challenges of puberty, you stand poised to explore its hidden paths, conquer its unclimbed peaks, and discover the treasures it holds.

But remember, this isn't a pre-determined map. No one can dictate the twists and turns your journey will take. The beauty lies in the unknown, the thrill of forging your own path, and the freedom to write your own extraordinary story.

So, how do you navigate this exciting wilderness? Here's your compass, adventurer:

Embrace your passions... Remember those things that set your soul on fire during puberty? Those sparks are the flames that will propel you forward. Nurture them, explore them, and let them guide you toward a life filled with purpose and joy. Whether it's art, music, science, or anything else that makes your heart sing, let your passions be your guiding stars.

Build your dream team; no adventurer conquers alone. Surround yourself with people who lift you up, inspire you, and believe in your dreams. These could be friends who share your laughter, mentors who offer wisdom, or even online communities that echo your interests. Remember, your tribe is your chosen family, the ones who celebrate your victories and hold your hand through challenges.

Embrace the bumps along the way, too. Life isn't always sunshine and rainbows. There will be moments of doubt, unexpected detours, and perhaps even some stumbles. But remember, even the strongest trees weather storms. Learn from your mistakes, pick yourself up, and use challenges as stepping stones to climb even higher.

Leave your mark on the world… Every individual has the power to make a difference, big or small. Whether volunteering in your community, standing up for what you believe in, or simply offering kindness to others, your actions can create ripples of change. Remember, even the smallest spark can ignite a fire that illuminates the world.

Never lose sight of who you are. As you explore new paths and encounter different experiences, never compromise your core values, or lose sight of the authentic you. Celebrate your individuality, embrace your quirks, and stay true to the principles that make you shine. This is YOUR adventure, adventurer, and only you get to decide how you live it.

This is important, lets go over it again.

- Exploring Your Passions: Remember those things that set your soul on fire during puberty? Whether it's art, music, writing, sports, or anything else that makes your heart sing, nurture those passions! They could lead you to exciting careers, lifelong hobbies, or even groundbreaking discoveries. The world needs your unique perspective and the magic you bring to everything you do.
- Building Your Dream Team: Surround yourself with supportive and inspiring people who believe in you and lift you up. These could be friends, family, mentors, or even online communities that share your interests. Remember,

your tribe is your chosen family, the ones who help you navigate challenges and celebrate your victories.

- Embracing Challenges: Life isn't always smooth sailing. There will be bumps on the road, moments of doubt, and unexpected detours. But remember, challenges are opportunities for growth. Learn from your mistakes, bounce back stronger, and never lose sight of your dreams.

- Making a Difference: You have the power to make a positive impact on the world, big or small. Whether it's volunteering in your community, standing up for what you believe in, or simply being kind to others, your actions can create ripples of change. Remember, even the smallest spark can ignite a fire.

- Living Authentically: Never lose sight of who you are at your core. Embrace your individuality, celebrate your quirks, and stay true to your values. Don't let anyone dim your light or pressure you into conforming to someone else's idea of who you should be. This is YOUR adventure, adventurer, and only you get to decide how you live it.

And finally, the most important things for you to remember…

The future is unwritten:

You have the power to shape your own destiny. Set goals, dream big, and take action toward your aspirations.

Embrace the unknown:

Don't be afraid to step outside your comfort zone and explore new things. The greatest discoveries often happen when we venture beyond the familiar.

Never stop learning:

The world is your classroom, and there's always something new to discover. Be curious, ask questions, and keep expanding your knowledge and skills.

Believe in yourself:

You are capable of achieving amazing things. Never doubt your potential, and remember, you are worthy of love, happiness, and success.

So, adventurer, get ready to embark on the next chapter of your incredible journey! With courage, curiosity, and a sprinkle of self-belief, you can navigate any obstacle and achieve anything you set your mind to. Remember, the future is yours to create.

CONCLUSION

This book was just your guide, a compass pointing you in the right direction, but the true adventure – your adventure – has just begun.

Remember the lessons you learned along the way: embrace your individuality, celebrate your passions, find your tribe, and never stop exploring. The future stretches before you, a vast landscape filled with uncharted territories, hidden treasures, and breathtaking vistas. Go forth, adventurer, with courage in your heart, curiosity in your mind, and an unwavering belief in your ability to achieve anything you set your sights on.

You carry the strength, resilience, and wisdom gained from your experiences. You have the support of your tribe, the magic of your individuality, and the limitless potential hidden within you. So, take a deep breath, adventure, and embrace the unknown. The world awaits your unique spark, your infectious laughter, and the incredible story you're about to write.

This isn't goodbye, adventurer. It's a "see you later!" Remember, the lessons you learned in these pages are yours to keep, a treasure chest overflowing with tools and wisdom you can use throughout your journey. So, whenever you face a challenge, need a reminder of your strength, or simply want to relive the laughter and growth of this incredible phase, come back to these pages.

SPECIAL BONUS

Want this bonus book for free?

SKILLS and be the first to claim a free download of our upcoming releases.

Scan the QR CODE   Join Today!

THANK YOU

Thank you for choosing our resource to support your child's growth; it means so much to us.

If you could take a moment to share your thoughts on Amazon or Goodreads.com, it would mean a lot to us and be a great help to other parents searching for trusted resources. Thank you.

Want to dive into the literary world before anyone else? Then join our Book Launch Club! As a club member, you'll be offered the opportunity to receive advanced copies of our upcoming releases directly to your inbox. All we ask is for you to leave honest reviews on Amazon.com and Goodreads.com. Your honest feedback will contribute to the book's success and help fellow readers make informed choices.

For more information on joining Skilled Fun's Book Launch Club skilledfun.com/book-launch-club or simply scan our QR CODE